the life & times of the

RICH $HOBO

by Allen L. Wellenstein

Printed and bound in the United States of America
First printing • ISBN # 978-0-9982386-3-0
Copyright © 2016

Cover photo courtesy *The Daily Interlake*

the life & times of the
RICH $HOBO

by Allen L. Wellenstein

For order information please call:
1-785-370-1085

SCOTT COMPANY PUBLISHING
P.O. Box 9707 • Kalispell, MT 59904
Toll Free: 1-800-628-0212
Fax: 1-406-756-0098

Dedication

Thanks to my Lord and savior Jesus Christ, King of Kings.

I dedicate this book to my mom, Carolyn Steide, the greatest mother a person could have. She is the rock of the family. She has seen a lot, and has been through some rough times, some good times. I have traveled all over the country, from the shore of San Diego, California to Seattle, Washington to Miami, Florida, to the flatlands of Texas and 12,000 feet up in the Rocky Mountains. I have hoboed all across the USA a couple of times over, but I still come back to Montana, just to see Mom again. She always has a warm, smiling face and is full of laughter and humor. God is flowing in that woman. She is kind to me and is a very good cook! She worried about me out there many a night, but said she put me in God's hands. I love you, Mom. God bless you.

Thanks also to my family and friends who made this book possible: Ralph Wellenstein, David Wellenstein, Nina Wellenstein, Larry and Darcy Fardett, Dennis and Deb McPherson, Guy and Jessie, Daniel and Shannon, my church family, Hope City and Fresh Life Church.

For all my investors and the people who have donated and bought flags. God bless you.

Me & Mom

Glacier National Park

Whitefish, Montana

Introduction

This is a real life story and it is mine – my travels, adventures, misadventures, mishaps, near death experiences, pain and suffering. My laughs, triumphs, miracles and experiencing God's healing right in front of me. I've eaten out of garbage cans and stayed at a fancy hotel in Seattle for free. I have ridden boxcars, flat cars and grain cars on the railroad. I have hitchhiked all over the country and seen 37 states, most of them by the time I was 20.

I toured with the carnival. I traveled from Florida to Washington just to see how long it would take – seven days to hitchhike and a few freight train rides. I still love trains but when I take them now, I have a seat. I am still a gypsy at heart; Nomad used to be my nickname on the street. I have been drunk and I am in recovery. I have taken so many drugs it would make your head spin and it is a wonder I have a brain left. I have been in two motorcycle accidents, five car accidents, two of them major, taken two falls off ladders and had three mental breakdowns. I have had so many vehicles over the years that I could be a used car dealer. I had so many different jobs and businesses you would hardly believe it. It is all here in this book.

When I was a teenager, I hung out with hobos, winos and beach bums who told me stories about traveling around. I wanted that life and to travel as much as I could, so when everyone else became a college student or got a job, I became a beach bum and hobo. After a couple of months of living on the streets I got used to it. That life gets in your soul and your very being. That's why I had to write this book – to let others know how it is out there and share my experiences, strengths and hopes, how people treat you when you're a street person, how many nice people are out there.

God bless and thank you for buying my book. Enjoy!

Mom & Me - 1964

Dad & Me - 1964

THE RUNAWAY

I remember my first hobo adventure was running away from home. I was born in Santa Monica and grew up in Escondido, California. I lived in the country when I was eight years old. My dad was a caretaker for an avocado orchard. He got free rent and he could cut down the dead avocado trees and sell the wood. He was strong, tough as nails. His hands were like steel. I felt them sometimes upside my head. I told my dad one night I was running away from home and to my surprise he said ok. I was kind of shocked and my mom did not like the idea.

Me - 1967

Dad knew what he was doing, in fact he might have done the same when he was a boy. I packed up my pillowcase with some clothes and took a sheet and a pillow. I did not know I was supposed to bring a sleeping bag or at least a blanket. I walked to my friend's house. His dad owned an orange grove. I could see my house on the hill. That made me long to go back home. I got cold and I was hungry after a couple hours. I was home sick. I did not realize at the time how blessed I was to have a house, bed and food, especially to have two parents that loved me. I came back that night realizing I needed a home, that I needed my mom and dad. How much I loved them. Dad knew I was going to come back. They were glad to see me and I was glad to see them too. I hugged them then got something to eat. My bed sure felt good that night. I was one happy kid.

It was like that story in the Bible about the prodigal son coming back from squandering his inheritance. He got to the point where he had to work in a pigpen feeding the pigs. He started eating what the pigs were eating. He said to himself, "I can go back to my father's house, I can be a servant or a hired hand, at least I will eat good." He started walking back to his father's house. He did not realize his father was looking for him. As he was walking toward his home, his father saw him far off in the distance. He started running towards his son, met him half way and hugged him. The father said, "My son was gone and now he has returned. Get me the best robe and put the ring on his finger. Get the fatted calf and cook it. Let's Celebrate." The prodigal son has returned. We do not have to run away any more. We get to run to the Lord today.

BIG HANDS

Old Dodge Power Wagon

Another time in my life, I was helping my dad in his wood business. I probably watched more then I helped, I was only six years old. The firewood pieces he cut up were bigger than me. It was fun to watch my dad work. He used to haul and deliver wood into the town of Escondido, California, where he sold it door to door. He drove an old Dodge power wagon that was built like a tank. There was no passenger door on my side, only a chain to hold on to. One time he turned the corner and I nearly fell out of the truck. I got scared because the ground looked so close and the truck was going pretty fast. I was hanging on to the chain so tight because I thought I was going to fall out. Without blinking an eye, my dad grabbed me and pulled me back into the truck. I was sure grateful for his quick reflexes.

That is how our Father in heaven is. We hold on to the world, things, money, etc. so tight just like I did with the chain. We should hold on to God that tight. Seek his kingdom first and all these things will be added unto you. God is always there to pull us back and to pull us up out of the pit that we dug for ourselves.

THE REBEL

When I was seven years old we used to burn trash. My mom told me, "Whatever you do, do not put that bottled hairspray in the fire." I did not listen as usual and put it in the burning trash. That hairspray bottle shot up in the air like a rocket. It went up about twenty feet in the air, came back down and lit the field on fire. I was running around and did not know what to do. My mom came out to see what I hollering about. She saw the

The Life & Times of the Rich Hobo

field on fire and got the hose to put the fire out. Luckily it was a small fire. Then my mother told me to go to the house. She whacked me a few times with her shower back scrubber, then forgave me for what I did. In fact, if I asked her today she probably would not remember 43 years ago. There are a lot of other things I have done to make her mad at me. She loves me, I know that today. I love her, too. Yes, I am a momma's boy.

Me - 1967

Our Father in heaven forgives in the same way. He doesn't remember any sin he put into the sea of forgiveness. We just have to forgive ourselves. That is the hardest thing to do, but we can with His help. We can do all things through Christ that strengthens us.

STEALING

I used to steal things that were not mine from my neighbors, friends and stores. I used to steal money from my grandmother. I think she knew but never said anything. I would go to the neighbor's and steal their ice cream. The ice cream was in the garage in the freezer and they never locked the garage so it was easy. My dad never used to let us eat junk food, candy, chips, cookies and cake, so that made me crave it even more. Not having something made me want to steal even more. Every time I stole I got scared and excited. The first time I stole something was at the health food store. I took a maple man in a box. If you don't know what a maple man is, it's a little man in a box, made out of pure maple sugar and they are very good tasting. They never caught me when I was a kid. It was exciting and I enjoyed it. I got caught stealing a lot when I got older. I felt bad years later when I found out it was a sin to steal. Fraud tastes good at first, then it winds up being a mouth full of grave.

BAD TEENAGER

When I was teenager, I ran away four or five times. Each time I ran away, when the police found me, they gave me back to my parents. They always were glad to see me. They missed me, and yes, they were worried about me. My father and mother always forgave me. My dad even had tears in his eyes one time at the police station. That is the way God is. He is a forgiving God and will forgive no matter how many times you run away. He loves you even more than your family and friends do. I regret being such a pain in the butt. I was doing so many drugs and running with the wrong people.

MAD TEENAGER

My mother was a very forgiving, loving and kind woman, but she did not put up with anyone's crap. There were a few times I saw the fire come out of that woman. One time there was a man in Arizona, where my dad had moved us all. A few business deals went bad and we had to move. The owner started giving us trouble and mouthing off. He said something to me and my mother got right in his face. She was not backing down. Her eyes turned red, she was boiling mad. She had gotten angry with me a few times. The last time she got real angry with me was the final straw. I came home one day, looked into the mirror and did not like what I saw. I was so angry that I punched the mirror, smashing it with my fist. Glass went flying all over the place. I cut my knuckles pretty badly, so there was blood all over the place. When my mother got home from work and saw the bathroom she was devastated, scared and angry. That was it, she'd had enough of me, so she called her brother, my Uncle Fred. He came over to the house and started yelling at me. I yelled back and then we got into it. We both had a temper and I think he was coming to knock some sense into me. We started fighting and wrestling. I had been working out with weights in jail so I was pretty strong, but I think Uncle Fred was stronger and I was not going to let him know that. We tore up the room pretty good. I don't know if the fight helped or not. I think it just made me more angry and resentful of my family. A couple of days later, my mother had to make the toughest decision in her life. I know that she still loved me, but she could not handle me, the drugs, alcohol, the police and the fights any more. For all the trouble I caused from the time I was 13 to 18 years old, I probably spent at least four years locked up in jail. They called it work camp Campo, California.

It was time to get out of the house. I packed up some clothes into the backpack I bought at Pick and Save. I threw the pack and a sleeping bag into Mom's car and she drove me to the edge of town and the ramp to the freeway. I think she knew I had hitchhiked before when I ran away. She pulled over and handed me $20. I can't remember what she said or what I said. I don't even know if we said anything at all to each other. That could not have been easy for her. From that day forward I did not have any family. I used to tell everyone my family abandoned me, kicked me out, disowned me. The road, tramps, hobos, winos, drunks, street people, ex-cons and bikers became my new family for seven years as I traveled all over the USA. I went back one time many years later when my brothers and I were all older. I visited for a couple of days and then was back on the road again. I didn't like hanging around for too long and was usually in trouble, but at least I had a family again. Today I realize I have a family in God's Kingdom. I got my new family in Christ on Easter Sunday in 2001. Lord Jesus will stick closer to you than a brother, no matter what. God will be there and never leave you or forsake you. He is your new family.

WORK

When I was growing up my dad beat into me that I had to work for everything. If I wanted money I had to work for it. My mother worked and my dad worked too, so I was asked to watch my brothers after school. I washed dishes and cooked for them for $25 a week, $5 for mowing the lawn and $5 for washing the car. I thought it was normal for everyone to take care of their

1965

My brothers

brothers at age 10, so I grew up very young and very fast. I was being responsible when I was supposed to be a kid. That made me hate hard work and is why I enjoyed hoboing so much. I never had to work, I just asked for or stole what I needed. If a hobo is working, then he is staying in one place and I hated that thought. Travel, travel – I love it.

I still had a good childhood. I learned how to ride a pony and a horse. I caught crawdads, pollywogs, frogs and lizards. When I was a kid I used to run pretty fast. I ran and jumped chairs just to see if I could do it. When I was in grade school I ran like the wind. I won ribbons and medals for the 50 and 100-yard dash, plus I won the pull-ups contest. Then I got to junior high school I started getting high. I was 12 years old when I smoked my first joint of marijuana. I was hooked. I was laughing at everything. I liked the feeling and I wanted more. I did more, all right. I did speed, cocaine, hash, LSD, heroine once. I wonder how I have a brain left. I drank a lot, too.

SCHOOL TROUBLE

I missed most of my junior high years because of my temper and also my smoking weed and getting so stoned. All I could do was stare at paper and the books, but mostly at the teacher. They had a teacher's aid in my class and she was so hot, but back to the story. We had school year round and I came back to the school although I was not supposed to be there. The coach said to me, "What are you doing here?" He said something else and then he pushed me against the wall and was shaking me. I hated teachers and coaches telling me what to do. I had a problem with authority. I exploded and started hitting him. I could not stop. Some teacher came to help get me off him. It took four teachers to pull me away. They dragged me off to the Principal's office. The cops showed up and took me to jail, then my parents came to pick me up.

I saw the judge a couple weeks later and he gave me 30 days in juvenile hall. After I was released from my 30-day sentence, I was not welcomed back to my previous school, so I had to go to probation school. The teachers were probation officers. If I got into trouble at this school, I would go back to juvenile hall. It was so much easier than regular school. I had smoke breaks, went to the bowling alley, watched movies. We still showed up stoned, I couldn't stay out of trouble. No matter how much trouble we cause for ourselves and others, our Father in heaven is forgiving. God will not turn his back on you. We are all saved by God's grace.

THE NEW LIFE

Before I started bumming around the country, I used to hitch rides to the beach. Some pretty wild people that used to party like I did hung out at the beach and lit party bonfires at night. I ran away one time when I was 15 years but I only stayed one night. The next day after spending all night partying, I was walking down the street to catch a ride when the cops pulled up. I had a pillowcase to carry everything on a stick to hold it. The cop told me I could not have the stick. It was illegal to carry, plus I was a minor and not allowed to hitchhike home, so they put me in jail until my parents came.

Probably three years later when I was out on my own and everyone else was going to college or finishing high school, I was learning how to be a beach bum. I looked good even though I was living on the streets. I was young and had a tan, long blonde hair and peach fuzz mustache. I attracted my share of women. I would swim in the ocean or wade and that would be my shower. I would eat out of dumpsters and beg people for money. I partied at the beach at night and sometimes I would pass out anywhere. When I first started living on the street or at the beach, there were times I got soaking wet from the rain. In the wintertime in California it rains all the time. I was a newbie to this stuff. I tried to sleep under a recliner chair. Then I use to sleep near the bathrooms. The rain would ruin any fire I built. Thank God for laundromats where I could dry my stuff out and stay warm.

On the weekends I learned how to ask for food at the beach. I got an Australian Shepard and Labrador mix dog I named Max. He was a smart dog. My dog and I were a good team when panhandling. I would ask people for change so I could get some dog food. People felt sorry for the dog and me, so they would give me some money. The dog used to eat crap when he was a puppy, so my friend called him Max, the shit eatin' dog. I used to get so angry when he said that. Another friend that I met bumming around had a big Saint Bernard that was so huge it looked like a miniature horse. One time we passed out on the beach we were so drunk, and forgot about the tide. We were in our sleeping bags when all of a sudden a wave of ice-cold water hit us. It was the high tide. That is a rude awakening, especially when you're hung over. We gathered all of our belongings and dragged them up to the fire to dry out and warm up. It was about 5 am too, so it was cold out. That goes to show you God's ideas are a lot different than our ideas. If we ask him for wisdom and knowledge he will give it to us abundantly. Thank God.

BOY SCOUTS

When my friend Dan and I were 15 years old we used to get stoned a lot. We needed money to get high and for other stuff like food, booze and cigarettes. We got an idea to dress up as Boy Scouts. He had a couple uniforms from his Boy Scout days so we put them on and went knocking on doors, asking contributors to send a Boy Scout to summer camp. Instead of doing it for a while then stopping, or even just going out once a week, we got greedy and did it three or four times a week. We were raking in some big money, at least we thought we were. It was free but there was a cost. After a few months we got caught. We knocked on the scoutmaster's door and they called the police on us. Further down the street the police stopped us and said we were under arrest for fraud and impersonating Boy Scouts. They told our parents that we were 15-year-old bunco artists and released us to them. This story shows if we were honest, we could have been good door-to-door salesmen.

I can only serve the Lord today. The love of money is the root of all evil. It is not money that is evil, but the love of it. We will do all kinds of crazy things to stack it up, save it, hoard it. I know from experience there is never enough. Money will not give you the peace that you deserve. Only the Lord Jesus Christ can do that.

DRINKING

A lot of crazy things happened in my teenage years, especially when I was drinking. I did drugs but I also drank often. One night there were four of us drinking beer, about two cases as we drove an old pickup truck into the hills of Escondido. Buzz was going fast around the corners, sliding sideways. He skidded the truck one way, then he would turn the steering the other way and hit the gas. There were no paved roads, just dirt, and dust was flying everywhere. We were all drunk, hooting and hollering, saying faster, faster! I blacked out and don't remember anything else from that night. When I woke up, I was hung over sick and my head was pounding. I was in the back of the pickup. Someone else was passed out next to me and the other two were passed out in the front seat. I looked around outside of the truck and saw we were parked on the edge of a hill. It went almost straight down, maybe a 100-foot drop from where the truck was. We could have all been killed that night. The Lord was watching over us even when we were ruining our lives. God is merciful. We are saved by his grace each day. He gives us our daily bread.

BIRTHDAY PARTY

My family had birthday parties for me but sometimes I did not show up if I was out drinking or doing dope with my friends. On my 16th birthday, I went to my friend's house instead of going home. His father bought us a keg of Olympia beer. There was music and a lot of drinking, and I hung around the keg. I got so drunk I passed out under the table where the beer was sitting. Some birthday that was. I woke up and started drinking again, then blacked out and don't remember anything except that when I finally came out of my black out, I had my hands around my friend's neck holding him up against the fence. I was never nice when in a black out. I never did good things, it was always trouble. I had many of them throughout my drinking career. Through Jesus Christ by his grace I have not had a drink since July 27th, 1987. Now when I have a birthday party, I can remember it. I have fun today. If you look at it one way, every day can be our birthday, every day can be a celebration.

THE WRECK

When I was 17 years old, my friend Buzz and I were on a motorcycle. It was a Honda 750 with a big engine and fast. It was a sunny day in San Diego on the freeway and we were going about 70 mph. The worst thing that could have happened, did. Our back tire blew out and we slid back and forth into one lane, then another. Thank God, we did not get hit or run over. Buzz finally slowed down to about 50 mph and had to lay the bike down. He got off the bike but I had my foot pinned under it when we finally stopped skidding. Someone helped us with the bike and the police came to take the report. For some reason the ambulance did not pick me up and take me to the hospital. The police car drove me home, then Buzz's dad came and picked him and the bike up. I was scraped up on my leg and arm, and my left heel was cut deep. Buzz's dad took me to the doctor the next day. The doctor said if I had been cut any deeper, I would have had a limp the rest of my life. I could have cut the tendons in my foot.

God was watching out for me again. Neither of us had been wearing helmets and I only had on a tank top, jeans and tennis shoes. We could have been killed. Years later I went to visit one of my old friends in Escondido and found out that Buzz had died in a car accident. He was one crazy dude. We did a lot of crazy things together. He lived life in the fast lane and outran the cops on that motorcycle. God rest his soul. I pray that he was saved before he passed, asked forgiveness of his sins before he left this earth. We all know the sinner's prayer. If anyone doesn't know it, but wants eternal life with their maker, just say to Him, "Lord Jesus I ask you into my heart and my life today. Forgive me of my sins. I will follow you, all the days of my life. Amen."

BEACH

At Moonlight Beach in Encinitas, California, there were always big bonfires blazing in the pit. We were all getting drunk, partying and feeling no pain, hooting and hollering like we often did. There was a lady named Cadillac Jean there who was one crazy woman. She used to get drunk every time she came down there, and this time she was so drunk she fell into the fire and started rolling around screaming. She was burned on her arm, hand and part of her leg, and it got some of her hair, too. She refused to go to the hospital and just kept on drinking. I don't think she left until the next morning. I was not too smart that night either. I passed out in my sleeping bag next to the fire pit. When I woke up the next morning I was hung over and sick, with 1,000 little holes in my sleeping bag. God watches over drunks and fools. I was both.

THE TRIP

As a teenager, I had taken small trips up and down the coast of California hitchhiking. When I was 18 years old, I went to Santa Barbara where I was introduced to the tramp and hobo life. I hung out with some real characters. They all had street names. There was a lot of drinking and drugs and eating out of dumpsters in the back of McDonalds and KFC. They would throw out the leftovers and it was good, sometimes even still warm. We would eat at the missions and the Salvation Armies to get a free meal. We slept in hobo jungles by the railroad tracks. Five or six of us would sleep in one area by the trees because there is safety in numbers.

I left Santa Barbara with a friend of mine to hitchhike across the country to some place in Georgia. There was going to be a bunch of hippies there, at a "smoke out." We parted ways in Barstow, but were supposed to meet up again in Georgia. I got stuck in Barstow for a couple hours before I finally got picked up by a guy driving a Cadillac to Las Vegas. When we got there, he stopped at a casino and gave me a few bucks to play the slot machines. Like a dummy, I trusted him and left my backpack, sleeping bag and jacket in the car. I went inside the casino and played a machine until I lost my money. When I came back outside I walked to the parking lot looking for the Cadillac, but it was gone. He had driven away with all my stuff, everything I owned. My heart just sank; I was too trusting. There I was stuck in Las Vegas in the middle of winter, wind blowing, cold, no jacket and broke with nothing but the clothes on my back. I walked around in the parking lot looking to steal a jacket out of a car. I just could not do it; I was not a good thief. I think someone gave me a jacket and sheet, something to eat. I was very good on the streets at begging or asking for things and people felt sorry for me. The jacket was a Levi with a wool liner on the inside, but it barely kept me from freezing to death. I also remember sleeping that night in a tunnel with the sheet over me. I don't think I slept very much.

I remember getting stuck in Flagstaff, Arizona. It was no fun to be stuck in the wintertime. It was snowing and bone chilling cold. It took us two days to get a ride out of there. We finally got picked up by a family that was going all the way to Albuquerque, New Mexico. I did not care how far they were going, just that the heater was on. They even bought us meals on the way. They were a Christian family, very generous people. When they dropped me off in Albuquerque they gave me some money to help get down the road. Still being a rookie, I found a shed out of the cold but soon I started itching. I did not realize it had fiberglass insulation on the floor. One itching night I couldn't stand it anymore so I went to a coffee shop. I got back to the on ramp and was picked up by some construction workers. They gave me their lunches and I was eating good homemade sandwiches.

I got picked up by a drunk in Mississippi. We found a little hole in the wall place to drink where I was the only white person. I was a little nervous but did not show it. We got drunk and didn't get in any fights, which was a miracle for me when I was drinking. I finally made it to Georgia. I landed in Atlanta but did not make it to the smoke out. It took me seven days and amazingly, I had money in my pocket, a new sleeping bag, a backpack and a nice big jacket. I realized the Lord was watching out for me. Even out there we don't have to worry about what we will drink, what we will eat or what we will wear. The Lord says pagans run after these things.

HOBO STEW

Hobo stew has a secret ingredient. It's called anything you can find. Sometimes we would find food to put in the stew from free places, dumpsters and stores, mix it all together in a big pot and boil it for a while. Most of the time it tasted really good. Sometimes we could not find any wood to have a fire to cook with, so we would use the old railroad ties with creosote on them. That's a chemical they treat the ties with and it kept them burning a long time. I don't think it was unhealthy for us.

STRANDED

I was stranded one time for two days in New Mexico when I could not get a ride. I ran out of water and had no food for the two days. What a place. The town did not want the homeless there, so I could not enter to get water or food. There are a lot of little towns and big cities that do not want street people in them or on the freeway either. Some places in the US will put you in jail for being homeless. There is a hatred toward homeless people in America that has to stop. It should not be illegal to be homeless. I bet Jesus and his twelve disciples camped out under the stars and sat around a few campfires. He even had to flee a few times.

THE LOSS

Another time in my life I was working in Atlanta, Georgia for a company called Labor Ready. I did not work one day so I went drinking and got so drunk the police picked me up for being drunk in public. The judge gave me 30 days in county jail. When they booked me before I went to the county stockade, I was in the city jail. I was the only white person and was nervous and a little scared but I did not let it show. One more time someone stole my backpack with all my clothes in it and my sleeping bag, so I had to start over again. When I started working for Labor Ready again, some other people and I were working for a demolition company and we moved to Tallahassee, Florida. We helped demolish the state capital building. The people I worked with all drank like fish. We made good money and they paid us for motel rooms and food. It was hard and dangerous work, so I worked hard and played harder. One night we were drinking all night and I drank myself sober, then we all passed out. They used to come pick us up at the motel to take us all to the job. The boss said they yelled at us really loud to get up, but we still did not wake up. All three of us got fired because I think we had past warnings.

We had one more day at the motel so I went to the beach that day. I was with a woman I met and we were having fun so did not care about anything. The bus dropped me off close to the motel but when I got there the door was locked. When I asked the motel clerk why, he said the people that were there took off. My heart sunk. All my clothes and other stuff, even a jar of change was gone. All I had to my name was a pair of shorts and a t-shirt, a pair of flip-flops and a towel. Even my wallet was stolen so my ID was gone, too. At least it was summer time in Florida. It was warm at night, so I found some cardboard and slept under a big tree. The next day I walked to the place where I used to work. I found my hard hat at the job site. I knew when I turned it in I could get $5. I told the boss my situation and he said he was sorry but could not do anything to help me. I was walking to the thrift store to buy some pants, maybe some shoes, when the flip-flops I had broke. There I was on the street with no shoes, no ID, $5 to my name. I was in bad shape. I did not have time to worry, I had to survive. At the store I had enough for a pair of pants, and some left over for a little food, smokes and a beer. I still had no shoes.

I went to the Salvation Army that night to see if I could get a bed and something to eat, but they said I could not stay without an ID. So I called Birdie, the girl I went to the beach with. I was almost crying when I told her my situation. She came to the park to meet me and was nearly crying too when she saw and heard how bad off I was. She brought some food to the park and I was happy about that, then she said I could stay with her and her brother. I found out he was in the carnival business. I met him and we got along well. He was a Jewish son from New York like his father. He asked if I wanted a job traveling around with the carnival. Since I still only had a t-shirt, pair of pants and a ball cap to my name, I said, " Hell, yes." I could not wait to get started. I guess I was not paying enough attention to Birdie. She brought someone home, started kissing him and they went to the bedroom. I took it pretty hard and felt hurt and angry. I never let her know about it, I just went out and got drunk. I think I borrowed some money from her brother Howard. I got so drunk that night I could not walk. I kept falling, so I got on all fours and crawled over the curb, across the lawn and up the stairs. I did not make it in the house so I passed out on the porch. A couple of weeks later I started working with the carnival. I was making more money than ever before. Howard used to tease me when he met me that I had no shoes on my feet. I still miss some of those carnival days. I could not take people for their money.

We have to remember God will bless us in the tough times as well as the good times. Our past does not equal the future. Our past is experience, strength and hope. I can realize how blessed we really are. I can be grateful I made it through the tough time. Thank God every day.

THE TWISTER

I was working the carnival at the Louisville, Kentucky state fair. It started off normal like any day at the carnival. People were having fun riding the rides, playing the games and walking around. The sky started turning a funny color I had never seen before. First green, then these black clouds formed in the sky. Some guy came running down the midway yelling that a tornado was coming. That was not a good thing to hear, so I tried to shut down the booth, close it up and tie it down. Then I stepped in some water in the booth as I tried to shut the lights off, and got a jolt of electricity like never before. Not smart. I left the lights on. I am very lucky I did not get electrocuted. The black cloud came at the carnival and everyone started running and screaming. The wind was picking up, then started howling like a freight train the closer it got. We were all running towards the stadium. A guy in a golf cart ran me over trying to get out of the way. I found shelter with some other people under the stadium for the football games. The storm tore the place up. Some booths and rides were not even touched, others looked like toothpicks. I went to the doctor's office and they wrapped up my foot. I had a sprained ankle, but because I was the carnival announcer, I could sit and do my work. I loved that part of the show, being an entertainer. The booth I had did not get damaged. The Lord was watching us that day.

DRUNKS AND FIGHTS

I got burnt out at the carnival. I was working so many hours, then traveling all over the country. I made good money but I spent it just as fast as I made it. I was a person from the streets and did not know how to handle money. Sometimes we would all get one room and stay there and shower; it was crazy. We were living like rock stars so I thought. Then sometimes I would be so broke, I slept on the carnival lot in the booth and we also slept in our cars. A lot of times we had to take funny little black pills or white pills to stay up extra hours, smoked weed and drank like fish. If I had all the money I blew in the carnival I would be a millionaire. One of my friends and I decided we had enough of the carnival business. We were in a college town in Texas and we both got overpaid. The boss did not like that, so off we went. We did what came natural, went to the bar and started drinking and talking to these guys who were brick machine operators, one of the toughest trades there is. We worked for them for a week, then we got paid. We got drunk as usual but then we had a fight and the little trailer we stayed in was torn up. The next thing we knew, four or five guys showed up. They kicked us out of the trailer and ran us out of town. Told us to never come back or there would be trouble.

THE GULF

I was in Galveston, Texas living on the streets. One day I was drinking beer and smoking weed. The woman who was with me said, "Let's go swimming," and I said ok. This was the Gulf of Mexico so there were all kinds of jellyfish, other strange creatures and fish. There was a sign out there in the water that said No Swimming Past This Point. Drunk and stoned, I ignored the sign. All of a sudden when I stepped down it felt like a shot of electricity on my foot. My hand went up in the air then I was swimming away from whatever stung my foot. When I put my foot down again I must have stepped right on it. It stung me with such force this time it felt like my foot was on fire. I started yelling and swimming like never before. The woman I was swimming with asked me what was wrong. I told her I got stung by a jellyfish. When I got onto the beach my foot was on fire, with tentacles stuck all over my foot and toes. To take the pain away I was drinking beer. I walked up the boardwalk and sat on a bench. I was pulling the tentacles off with a popsicle stick and someone put meat tenderizer on my foot. They said it would help, but then my foot started blistering and swelling up. It felt like 1000 bee stings. A guy came by to see what was going on and said I did not get stung by any old jellyfish. "You got stung by a man-o-war, a giant jellyfish with a lot of tentacles." He told me, "Get in the truck, I am taking you to the hospital. You will lose the foot if I don't." So I got a shot at the hospital and some cream for my stings, plus they gave me some crutches, too. I don't want to go through that ever again.

GALVESTON, TEXAS

I was walking with my crutches along the streets with my backpack and sleeping bag. My life was in the backpack and sleeping bag. I was getting hungry so I thought I would stop at a restaurant on the beach. I opened the door with my backpack on and started to set it down. The owner of the place said, "Hey, your backpack stays outside." I was not going to put my backpack outside. I asked him if I could leave it there. He rudely said, "Hell, no." I said, "Go screw yourself," and I don't think I said it that nicely either. You get the point. I slammed the door then called him a few other names on the way out. I made it across the street but he called the police on me, so they took me to the station for disorderly conduct. I looked at it like rest and food. I did not always eat well on the road or the streets. I was there for seven days, and they fed us from the restaurant next door, three times a day. One drunk guy started mouthing off to them, so they put his head between the bars and closed the door. After they hit him about four times he fell on the floor. The cops gave me a ride to the edge of town. They told me to never come back or they would put me in jail every time they saw me. So I believed them and haven't been back since.

AUSTIN, TEXAS SHOWER

I was in Austin, Texas and we had been drinking all night. We got so drunk we passed out in the park in our sleeping bags. Everything was fine until the sprinklers came on about 3 am. That will sober a person up quick. What a rude awakening. That got us right up out of a dead sleep. Everything was wet and we were soaked. We sure were not happy. The joys of living on the streets. I have not slept in a park since that night.

OUTLAWS AND POLICE

When I used to travel, it was safer to travel with someone. In a lot of my stories, there is usually someone else in it too. A guy I met in a bar in Austin, Texas became a friend of mine, so I thought. He kept a little secret from me. He never told me he was an outlaw wanted for a murder in the state of California. One night we were drinking boilermakers and got so drunk we fell down a hill and passed out. When I woke up I was in a pile of leaves next to a tree that stopped my fall. He was about ten feet below me on the hill. Even then the Lord was watching over me. I could have killed myself rolling down that hill. He comes to you right where you are. You don't have to wait until you get it all together. Come as you are.

We started hitchhiking up to LaCrosse, Wisconsin. He had family there and said there was work, so I said, "Let's go." After three days we finally got there and stayed with his girlfriend. That night we drank again and I blacked out. I didn't remember anything. The next morning we got a campsite and of course kept drinking. One afternoon a couple of days later, my friend and his girlfriend, his sister and I were at the campsite when all of a sudden there was a noise like I had never heard before. About ten different police forces showed up. Federal cops, sheriff's department, state troopers and local police were skidding their tires and drawing their guns.

They had shotguns, pistols and rifles and were cocking hammers back; they were not messing around. They were shouting and yelling to get on the ground. They said, "If you even move a muscle, we will shoot you dead." I have never had that many guns drawn on me at once. I was scared. We got into the car and went to jail. They kept asking about a murder in California. I found out the cops thought I was a suspect in the murder. The police took my statement and my story. After a week they decided they had a lack of evidence and it was a case of mistaken identity. The police told me when I was in a black out that my friend stole some guns and shot a telephone pole.

When I got out of jail they said they never wanted to see me in La-Crosse, Wisconsin again. The cops had taken my big jacket and when I asked them where it was, they said they would look for it. I just let them have it. I stayed the night at the Salvation Army and the next morning I was gone. Never went back. The enemy will accuse us of all kinds of things. But don't listen to him. He is the father of lies. He is a liar, cheat and a thief. We get to put the armor of God on today.

THE MISSED TRAIN

Another time I was riding a freight train from El Paso, Texas to Tucson, Arizona. There were three of us and it was my turn to get the water. We were riding in a boxcar, so I got my backpack off the train to go get the water. I turned around to look at the train for some reason and saw it was taking off. I was angry because I was stranded in the middle of nowhere. I started walking and finally got to the freeway. I am glad I missed that train. I found out later that it derailed on the way to Tucson. One of the tramps died and one broke his back in three places. One more time the Lord had saved me.

FIGHT IN THE PARK

God was watching over me again. I was living on the streets in Port-land, Oregon. At the park by the river, four or five of us were drinking as usual. I think it was wine, the cheap stuff that tastes bad and gets you so drunk so quick – Thunderbird, or as the street people call it, Thunder Chicken. Some other people showed up to share with us and we had more wine. You get too many people together drinking, there is bound to be a fight and trouble. Sure enough a fight broke out. The next thing I knew there were people running around the park with knives, and someone had an ice pick. I think I was trying to protect myself, plus I did not have a knife to fight back. Six people were stabbed; I was the only one that was not. God watches over us, even when we are running, drinking and stealing.

THE YELLING BUSH

In the Bible there was a burning bush. In this book there is a yelling bush. I use to sleep in some bushes next to a church by the sidewalk. It got noisy sometimes. There was a bench on the corner where people would sit, talk, laugh and party. I would lay there and listen to them, and sometimes I would grumble. There were other times I would yell at them, tell them to shut up because I was trying to sleep. The people would get real quiet and then they would leave real quick because they were scared that some angry homeless person started yelling at them from the bushes. I just thank God every night that I don't have to yell at people from the bushes anymore.

THE HOT TUBS

A bunch of hobos and I used to be caretakers for a place on the Kern River, just outside of Bakersfield, California. We took care of the place, kept it clean, picked up all the trash, beer bottles and cans. A lot of people came to the parties, drinking and smoking weed. There were natural hot tubs where a natural hot spring came out of the ground. Clothing was optional and there were a lot of loose women. I had quite a bit of fun in those days. It was only during the wintertime because the weather was too hot in the summer and there were too many crazies. One night some crazy guy came down there to the hot tubs with a gun, then he started yelling and shooting. I think he had a .38 or .45. A bunch of us hid in the bushes and some of us got on the ground. I was pretty scared. A lot of us were hippies. We did not carry guns. One of my friends was in Vietnam, so he went into combat mode. Someone called the police and about ten of them showed up, found the guy and arrested him. Sometimes the Lord sends angels to encamp around you, and to watch over you in your times of trouble.

DAISY PAINTED TRAILER

I had just gotten done with a carnival spot in Saint Louis, Missouri. We were driving to Florida to sell some mirrors and on the way we stopped at a gas station. There was a travel trailer at the side of the station with a for sale sign on it. They wanted $700 but we talked them down to $500. The only problem it had was they had painted the trailer full of daisies and flowers all over the trailer. Plus it was red and stuck out like a sore thumb. It was embarrassing. We took the trailer all the way to Miami. People were laughing and pointing. Some people loved it and others just went wow. We loaded the trailer and station wagon full of mirrors. The mirrors were heavy for the trailer. All of a sudden the car blew a back tire out and the trailer swerved into the left lane, then the right lane, fish tailing all over the freeway. I hit the brakes just a little and finally got it stopped. Luckily there was no traffic. We could have gotten into a horrible accident. We made it to Miami, unloaded the mirrors and unhooked the trailer. We spent two days at the flea market selling them and I made a lot of money. The space where we parked the trailer was across the street from an old Jewish man, someone Howard knew. After selling the mirrors I went and got drunk. The next day I started painting that ugly flower trailer silver. I think it took two coats to cover those daisies up. One night I was trying to fix the lamp and reached inside the cover for the light. There $750 all rolled up in 20-dollar bills. Wow, was I shocked. Somehow down the road I got screwed out of the trailer, or maybe I just gave it to Howard. The Lord blesses us in the same way sometimes. Through all of our trial and tribulations, He blesses us. He always turns bad things into a blessing or for good.

THE PAST, NO REGRETS

With some of the crazy things I have done in my life, I can't count the cost, especially when I was drunk or saying the heck with everything – leaving and running, going to a new place, new town. Problem is I took myself on those trips and runs. Even in a new place, there I was, everywhere I went. I can't afford to have any regrets, only memories, that is why I am writing these stories. I could write another book on past mistakes. One time I was in Fort Worth, Texas, all set up to go to welding school. I had all the grants, financial aid, books and everything. I went out and got drunk and blew it off, never went back. I don't know why I did not go in and apologize to the person in charge. I guess I was too ashamed to go back. I thought my girlfriend at the time was going to kill me. Thank God the Lord forgives us for our past mistakes, even the mistakes and blunders we make today. God will forgive us, if we ask him. We have to learn how to forgive ourselves though. That is the hardest thing to do.

LONELY CHRISTMAS

One time as I was hitchhiking across the country, I walked along the freeway trying to get a ride. It was impossible. It was Christmas Eve and no one was out driving that night. I looked off into the distance and saw a house with all the lights on. The window curtains were open enough to see the people having dinner, celebrating Christmas. In that moment in time I became so lonely. All alone, just me and the road – that is the way it was at the time. I did not stay lonely for long. You can't survive when you are lonely and feeling bad about yourself. I had God in my life, but not like I do now. Like with a friend, I am still learning how to be a friend. It was about 9:00 pm and started snowing, so I knew I had better find some shelter. I found a rest area with some trees behind it. I snapped limbs off of the pine tree and built a snow shelter with a tarp over the limbs. That night it snowed about six inches. The shelter was warm, like inside an igloo. I always traveled with two sleeping bags. One was a down mummy bag, the other was a regular sleeping bag. They kept me warm and dry and from freezing to death quite a few times. It was Christmas that morning when I came out of the snow shelter. Some people were sitting at the tables having hot chocolate. They asked me where I came from. I told them I built a snow shelter behind the rest area. They were amazed and offered me some hot chocolate. I wondered how I did not freeze to death out there on the road sometimes. I just knew how to survive in the train yards, hobo jungles, streets, boxcars, bridges, fields, abandoned houses and tents. So when people ask, "Do you want to go camping?" I say, "Hell, no."

Instead of just surviving now with Jesus Christ, we get to thrive. If I go somewhere these days, I take a train with real seats or I get to fly or drive a vehicle, see the sights. It is a great life. I don't get lonely as much any more.

LADY IN THE PARK

I was in a park in Tacoma, Washington, sitting on a bench when a little old lady sat down next to me. She was all wrinkled up. There was not a space on her face that did not have a wrinkle. I found out why – she was 109 years old and still walking in the park. She was still independent. I was amazed. Boy did she tell me some stories from her past. She was in the Second World War. They called women who were active in World War II "WACsies." In some stories in the Bible people lived a long time, 120 to 145 years old. I have never again met anyone that old. She had a lot of wisdom and knowledge.

THE MAN WITH A SHOPPING CART

When I was only 19 years old I was living in Portland, Oregon. I was hustling the streets to get alcohol, food and cigarettes. I never thought of a place to stay except those nights when it was cold and raining and the wind would blow. I had lived there for six months and only saw the sun maybe three days and the rest of the time it rained and rained. I panhandled on the streets, which is asking for money. I sold balloons at the park. One time I even got a shopping cart and started picking up cans and bottles. The Navy was in the port and they liked to drink. So for about a week I was picking all their cans and bottles up, sleeping in an abandoned house. As usual I drank all the money up. After the Navy left town I left the shopping cart, there was no money in it after that. It seems like even when I had nothing living on the streets, I always made money; maybe that's why they gave me the name "the rich hobo." That is a God given gift. Even when I was a kid, especially when I started working I knew how to save it up. We can serve only one God today. It is not money.

TROUBLE IN FORT WORTH, TEXAS

In Fort Worth, Texas I had been drinking all day. Jim Beam whiskey was my favorite, that and anything else. I blacked out like I usually did when I drank too much, which was most of the time. I did not know when to stop. That night I staggered home. I fell into the gutter. I was so drunk I could not get up so I decided just to go to sleep. Cops came by and stopped, threw me into the car. Being that there were women cops, I was giving them all kinds of trouble, calling them names, asking if they wanted to go to bed with me. They got me to the station and beat my ass and did not leave a mark on me. Then male cops got a hold of me. They beat me, too and did leave a mark on me. I got out the next morning. They released me for time served for being drunk and a public nuisance. I could not work for a week after they let me out because of the beatings. I never mouthed off to any cops after that. I said, "Yes sir, yes ma'am. "

THE BOSS WITH A GUN

Another time I was drinking too much again. Seemed to be a pattern here. We had been drinking beer all day. Our boss did not pay us for the work we did all week. We got pissed, we were ready to jump on him and take our money. He pulled a gun out on us. Told us to step away from him or he would shoot us. We backed away. He finally paid us. The next night we met at one of our friend's house down the street. We were drinking, getting louder and louder. Finally he said something, I said something and the fight broke out. He forgot he pulled a gun on me the night before. I was so pissed. I beat him pretty badly, then I picked him up and threw him in the back of the pickup truck. Thank God the Lord forgives us, so many times. He is not angry with us. We are to live slow to anger. Fast to listen and slow to speak. I have to remember that daily. I am going to put in my wallet.

TWO THIEVES ON THE HIGHWAY

I sure dodged a bullet this one time. Or God was looking out for me again. I was on highway 40 hitchhiking. I got picked up by these two characters. They were like Beavis and Butthead on crack, talking fast and stealing everything that was not nailed down. They stopped at some place and stole tools from a big rig truck. I saw the writing on the wall. These guys were going to get into trouble. I did not want to be there when they did. I said to them, "Hey let me off at the next exit." So they did and I was glad to get out of that car. They also told me they were driving around the country stealing. I always thought stealing was bad karma. I stole from the store sometimes when I was hungry. Well sure enough, someone picked me up and gave me a ride ten miles down the road. I was standing on the on ramp when I looked up and saw those guys I got a ride with. Six cop cars were chasing them. I was thanking God I was not in that car.

ON THE BICYLCLE

One time I was riding my bicycle home at night because I could not get a ride. I came out of the driveway of the house where I had been and heard a siren way out into the street. When I looked to the left to see where the siren was coming from, I saw I was in the middle of a high-speed chase. A car was speeding right towards me and the police cars were chasing after it. I was terrified, I have never peddled a bicycle so fast. In fact I know God gave me strength to peddle the bicycle fast so I would not get hit. I would have been splattered all over the road.

WILD HORSES

Another memorable time I was in Missoula, Montana. My brother Ralph and I were doing an asphalt job. We were taking a break, getting some water when I looked off in the distance. Western Montana is all hills and mountains. Coming up over the hill was a herd of wild horses running full speed. There must have been 25 or 30 of them. They ran through the pasture and back up the next hill and just like that they were gone. I was awestruck. It was one of those once in a lifetime moments, a Kodak moment. My brother was amazed, too. These moments are God's glory to us. That is why I am writing this book, to share those memories with you.

HUMOR

We have to laugh about life and all the crazy stuff that happens to us. We get to choose to be happy. Humor helps a lot, especially when life is handing you lemons. I make lemonade, put some sugar in it and sell, sell, sell it. Sold is my favorite word. Plus, it is easier to sell things when you have humor. It makes life fun and happy. I have found that the Lord Jesus helps, too.

MOTHER'S CAR

When my brother Ralph and I were in Fallbrook, California, I borrowed my mother's car, a little 1970 Chevette. We were both drunk, drinking and driving. We drove up to a place on top of a hill with a big flat surface. I hit the gas and that little car moved fast. We started spinning left then right. Then we started spinning the car around in circles in the dirt. We created so much dust in the air I could not see any more. I stopped the car. We were right on the edge of the hill that dropped straight down. We could have been killed that night, injured or wrecked the car. Mom would have killed both of us. The Lord saved both of us from any harm that night.

THE FLYING TRUCK

When I lived in Fort Worth, Texas I did a lot of construction and labor work, but mostly roofing. I made some good money roofing. I worked for a contractor who was a drunk big time. We got run off of more jobs. He must have been a good talker or a good line of bull. He always had work, but sometimes we messed jobs up. We were trying to fix a door but we just made it worse. The guy that we were working for yelled at us to stop the job and called us a bunch of butchers, wackos and bums. One day we were getting drunk and had been drinking beer all day. His name was Guy. He said, "I don't want this camper on this truck anymore." We had a brilliant idea. We had those brilliant ideas when we were drunk. So our idea was to drive the truck through the back alley as fast as it would go and hit the pile of dirt that was piled up there. So he said, "Let's do it," and of course I said, "Yes, let's go for it, sounds good to me." We took off at full speed, about 60 mph and hit that dirt mound. We were flying, all four wheels were off the ground. It was something you would see in the movies. When the truck hit the ground, the camper slid off. After we got our bearings we picked up all the tools that were scattered all over the place. We got the hell out of there before cops showed up and left the camper there. Luckily we did not get hurt. I think he did mess the truck up. Talk about the crazy things we do when we are drinking.

THE MONTANA ADVENTURE

I went on a trip of a lifetime. It was not Australia or an African Safari or Hawaii, but those are on my bucket list. It was in the middle of the winter of 1993. I was in the cab business in Sacramento, California, leasing from Co-op Cab Company. I was doing pretty well, but as usual I had hair up my backside or as my grandfather called it, itchy feet. He was a rolling stone, too. It runs in the family, plus my girlfriend gave me a good excuse to take off. I got pissed off at her so I left the state. We broke off our engagement – that might have had something to do with it. So I sold everything at the flea market and left the rest. I didn't even tell the taxi company I was leaving. I never liked saying goodbye. I was used to sneaking out the back door. After I sold everything, I took off on the road in my old 1976 Monte Carlo. It ate a lot of gas, but it was a good cruiser with a good engine. I left with $50 in change and $80 in cash from the sales. I am more of a saver now than I was then, when I didn't save anything. I drove to Nevada and went north on Hwy 45 or Hwy 98. That old windy road went all the way up to Montana. I slept in my car all the way there. I am spoiled now, I get a motel anytime I can when I'm driving or traveling. I got a speeding ticket in a little town in Idaho. The highway I took wound up through the mountains with beautiful scenery.

I made it into Columbia Falls, Montana. I stayed in a trailer with no heater and no bathroom in the middle of winter. I am from California and this was Montana. It was freezing and snowing. I was there a week and found some work cutting and stacking Christmas trees on a Christmas tree farm. It was the hardest work I have ever done. It was back breaking so after about two weeks I had to quit. The owner was not happy I could not handle it anymore. I was driving around in town and it had just snowed. I did not know how to drive in the snow. The car in front of me hit his brakes, I hit mine and went sliding sideways right into a bus. I helped my stepfather and mother paint a house, and after the painting was done it was time for me to go. I was missing the taxi business and my ex-girlfriend, so I took off in the afternoon. I drove down to Hwy 15 south to Salt Lake City, Utah. The more I drove the more snow started falling. I was driving in a blizzard and could not see where I was going. The big rig trucks were the only thing that kept me from going off the road. On top of everything I had bald tires. Talk about white knuckle driving. I drove like that all the way to Salt Lake. I sure was glad to get through my first time driving in a blizzard. I got something to eat and got back on the road. I was pulled over by the police in Elko, Nevada. I have had problems there in the past. The cop gave me a ticket and almost took me to jail and impounded the car, but I talked him out of it. When I finally got to Sacramento, California, I asked the taxi company if I could lease the cab from them and they said, "Sure, next time before you leave, tell us. We thought you were dead." Another crazy trip when I know God watched over me shaking his head. Friends of mine say I have two angels watching over me, probably more. I need them, even today.

LIFE AND ALMOST DEATH IN THE TAXI

As you may have noticed, I am a man of many hats. I drove a cab from 1994 to 1999 in Sacramento, California. I drove for all the taxi companies at one time or another. I worked days, nights and weekends. When I was driving and BS-ing with the customers, I was making easy money. That is why I did it for so long, I loved it. Like most businesses there were parts of it I hated. That all came to a screeching halt one night about 3:30 am in the morning when I got into a horrible accident. I put gas in the taxi at a station and got back onto the freeway, on the ramp of Hwy 50 going east. As I came up over the bridge, I-5 split into the off ramp. I did not see the accident in front of me or just blacked out. The accident was so horrific, my mind blocked it out. There was a big two-ton delivery truck on its side in the middle of the freeway. A van was smashed into the truck, the Highway Patrolman. I was traveling at 65 mph when I crashed into the scene of the accident. They said I did not even hit the brakes. The front of the car was smashed right up to the doorframe. Some of the engine came through the floorboard. I bent the steering wheel, the front windshield broke on my arms and the dashboard was smashed against my chest. The firefighter had to cut the dashboard and cut the top of the car off just to extract me out of the cab. I went into shock and blacked out again. I don't remember the ambulance ride. Unfortunately I do remember them cutting my clothes off in front of God and everyone.

The next thing I remember I was in the ER trauma unit. I was in so much pain; I had never felt pain like that. I wanted pain medication badly, but they do not give it right away. The doctors wanted to make sure I didn't have any internal bleeding. They did not give me any water either, just a wet sponge to drink from instead. The doctors and nurse took my blood, they did MRI's and CAT scans. Finally they gave me some morphine. I was in so much pain, but at least it was bearable with the morphine. My right big toe was broken and the doctor had to rebreak it. When they pulled my boots off my toe came out crooked. They did not get it right the first time, it took another try. They said that one of the things that saved my life was I had steel toed boots on. I was probably the only cab driver that wore steel-toed boots. The way the engine came through the floorboard, it smashed into the boots. Without them they said I would have bled to death. Plus I was wearing my seatbelt. The Highway Patrol said if I had not been wearing it, they would have scraped me off of the back of the truck. Angels were watching over me that night. It took the firefighter two hours to cut me out of the cab. I was hurting badly. I had bruises all over my legs. My elbows looked like someone stuck golf balls in there. My arms and hands were all cut up, with pieces of glass in them. The left side of my head had a cut on it. My nose had some skin gone from it. I had three cracked ribs and a bruised sternum. To this day I can still hear my sternum cracking. I had a broken toe. I broke the top part of my foot and fractured my leg at the knee. I had a big gouge on my left shinbone. I was in UC Davis Medical in intensive care for one day and trauma care for three days. I was not bleeding or dying so they kicked me out. That is their policy. I used to give the nurses a hard time – most of them were idiots, though some were nice, too. I also remember the morphine made me think I loved everyone. The Lord had his angels around the taxi that night.

THE LOST YEAR

I went home with a soft cast, crutches and a hand full of gift cards. I was amazed how many people called and came by to visit me in the hospital. They also gave me a bottle full of Vicodin, a very powerful pain medicine. I had to take it every four hours but I usually took it about every 3½ hours because the last ½ hour I was in so much pain. I started breaking them up into a powder form so it would take the pain away quicker. My friend came over to visit me and said I was in no shape to take care of myself, so they let me stay at their house for about four days. I needed help just to get up from the chair. I stood up on the porch, but was on so much Vicodin, I tipped over. I fell on a brick and landed on my back and neck. The doctor x-rayed my back and said there was a hairline chip in my vertebrae. That was all I needed on top of the other injuries. I was a mess. I finally got back home. I still could not completely take care of myself. I found out who my friends were real quick. They gave me rides to the store, to the doctor, even my ex-girlfriend came over a few times. People cooked for me, mowed my law and brought my food over. I was on crutches for four months. I had to walk with the crutches but no cast for three months. It was a battle from the time I got into the accident until a year later, physically, financially and spiritually.

The battle started in the ER in the hospital. The man who owned the taxicab that I leased came to the hospital and told me the vehicle only had a salvage title, so he did not have full coverage on the cab. He'd had the cab crushed, I think to get rid of evidence but I could not prove it. I went to file for workers comp for my medical bills. They said I was off the clock, so they wouldn't pay for my hospital bill. They said to go to a low cost Salud Clinic in Sacramento instead. Plus I made the mistake of hiring a lawyer that the owner of the cab referred me to, so there was a conflict of interest. I was in the fight of a lifetime. I was living off my savings, which dried up after six months of not working. I had to cash in my IRA just to eat, make my rent and car payment, all while trying to recover physically. On top of everything, the hospital was suing me for $60,000 for four days in their hospital. It is expensive to keep you alive. Then my lawyer was giving me the run around, so I had to fire him and hire another lawyer. I was suing the cab company. Workers comp was battling with me. Then the IRS came after me for cashing in my IRA. They sent me a nice bill. I was ready to have a nervous breakdown. Plus I had another lawyer trying to sue the guy that caused the accident. I was running out of money. Then I started having nightmares. I kept getting flashbacks of the accident. I would be thinking about the dash against my chest and start crying.

I finally went down to Salud Clinic mental health, where they asked me some questions. When they asked me if I felt like committing suicide, I said no, but did think about parking my car on the railroad tracks and waiting for the train to see what would happen. They said that was suicide. They put me in the front of the line and scheduled a doctor. They gave me some Prozac, which helped a lot. I had a rough time of it. I had to go to rehab for my leg and foot, because one leg was big and the other one was skinny. I had to learn how to walk again and it was very painful. I had run out of money so I had to go on welfare. I was ashamed at first. I had not been on welfare in a long time. When I was bumming around the country, I used to get food stamps – we called them tramp stamps. The welfare place held interview classes and computer classes. They gave me a few bucks for my next job, so I bought a pair of new shoes. I had recovered from my injuries and finished the painful rehabilitation. I found my first job and while it was not a dream job, it was a job. I was a dishwasher at Denny's in West Sacramento on the night shift. It paid the bills and provided free food. It was the hardest work I ever did, all through my pain and suffering, the rehab, the trials, battles with all the legal stuff, fear.

I felt like it was almost over, that I was coming out of the tunnel. There was a light at the end and it wasn't a train. When I was in the middle of the battle, I started going to a Bible study on a guy's boat. His name was Captain Bob. Then I was watching Oral Roberts on TV. He was talking about Jesus and how people got healed and saved. One day my friend Anne took me to church. I heard the message. I liked what the preacher said. I went a few more times, then did not go back for a while. Then my youngest brother Ralph came down from Montana. He was so happy, a different person. He gave me his testimony, what Jesus had done in his life. A week after he left and went back to Montana, I went to church that day. The Holy Spirit was moving. I felt something I had never felt before. The pastor asked if anyone there wanted to give their heart to the Lord today. Something on the inside of me jumped. I walked to the front of the church. I prayed the sinner's prayer with the pastor. I started crying, asking for forgiveness for my sins. I also cried for joy. I am saved now. I told everyone I knew how good the Lord Jesus is. The hospital called me up and said they were canceling my $60,000 debt. Then I got a job with a shuttle company. The first month I worked there I made $3,000. Then I got paid $30,000 for all the legal battles.

The accident was the best thing that ever happened to me. The Lord saved my life that night in the cab for a reason. Jesus gave his life for me and you. I give him my life every day. You can do the same if you have not given your heart to Christ. He loves you right where you are. He will clean you up inside and outside. Just say Jesus I ask you into my heart. Forgive me my sins. I will follow you all the days of my life. In Jesus' name, Amen. Welcome into the Kingdom of Heaven. He will never leave you or forsake you.

THE FLEA MARKET

I was living in Fort Worth, Texas. My two friends and I were at the flea market that day, looking at the stuff that people were selling. It was hot and

The Life & Times of the Rich Hobo

muggy, and like any other summer day in Texas, it was a little cloudy, too. I looked up and all of a sudden it got dark and off in the distance the sky was green. There was an eerie stillness in the air. The temperature dropped. There were no birds in the air. My friend looked at us said, "Let's get out of here." We all knew that there was a big storm brewing. One of my friends had to walk on crutches. His legs were like jelly. He was paralyzed from the waist down. His arms were his legs – they were huge. By the time we got to the car it was thundering and lightening. It started hailing stones the size of rocks. I thought they were going to break the windshield. The wind started blowing so hard it was rocking the car up and down like there was an earthquake. We could not see anything but hail stones and wind. I was not scared either; I thought it was exciting. We were all drunk, too. I don't think the vendors or the people in the flea market thought it was exciting. That storm tore that flea market up and the city, too. A bowling alley's roof collapsed because of the weight of the hail. Car lots were damaged. People could not drive. We all got excited and started chasing the storm, driving around in it. I was drunk as usual but it was still fun.

I have loved storm chasing ever since. I have watched some wild storms up in Montana, and in Michigan working in the carnival. Back then I did some crazy things. Even today we do some crazy things. God will take care of us in the storms of our lives. He will stop the storm in our life. He will say, "Ye of so little faith."

THE LITTLE CAR

There was another time that God was watching over me again. I was living in Fallbrook, California and one night I was driving on the street in two-lane traffic. I made a left hand turn and was sitting in the middle lane. I looked in my rearview mirror for some reason and saw a Toyota truck coming at me full speed. I braced myself for the crash. He crashed into my little 1980 Chevrolet Chevette going about 50 mph. He smashed up the back of my car pretty bad, plus when he hit me it knocked my car into oncoming traffic. Luckily no one was there. The wrecker came and towed my car to my apartment. The next day I walked to a friend's house and I asked her for a ride to the hospital because I was in so much pain. I found out I had whiplash from the car accident. They gave me muscle relaxers, which were Valium and something for the pain. I was in recovery but it still felt good. Yes, I did take them for the pain. When the pain was gone I stopped taking the pain pills. I was in a neck brace for a month. My stepfather came over to the apartment and fixed my car enough to be drivable. He pulled the bumper away from the tire and that way I could drive it. The crash bent the frame, too. The frame was a unibody – the car was the frame – so now it drove crooked. The insurance company and two garages said the car was totaled and the lawyers got me $8,000. The lawyers were paid $3,000 so I got $5,000. I was not very good with my money back then. I probably spent it on a lot of junk I did not need, like a new pair of boots or new hat.

The car had been my mother's for a while and I used to borrow it. Before the major accident, another person and I got into a fender bender or small crash, but we just scraped each other's paint. We called it even and went our separate ways. When I got home I told my mom about the accident. She said, "Well, since you have scratched my car you might as well buy it." We both agreed and she sold me the car for $300. That car went through a lot and still kept running. My brother broke out the back window when he was putting his bike in the car. Then in the major car accident the other window was smashed, so one day I decided to break the rest of them out. I cut the top of the car off up to the front seats and took the back seats out. I built a cab out of plywood and sheet metal and made a little truck. It did not look bad either. The car did have a few problems. One of the flywheels only had a few teeth on it, so when I would try to start the car, it would make a horrible screeching sound. It was so embarrassing. I finally sold it to my brother Ralph for $200 and about eight hours of labor on a roofing job. He built a wood camper on the back of the car. The problem was it was so heavy it nearly busted the springs. He got pulled over a few times in it by the police. For almost a year it was running on three cylinders because I stripped one of the spark plug holes, oops. I think it finally died, and my uncle Fred buried it. I think we are a lot like that old car. We get battered and bruised, broken up in life, but we still keep going. God accepts us just like we are. He said, "Come to me all who labor and are heavy laden and I will give you rest." Our yoke is heavy, His is light.

RECOVERY

I used to drink a lot. I drank to get drunk, hammered, blasted, plastered, stoned – you can call it what you want. I hated life without drinking. I loved to drink. I was an alcoholic. I could not live without it, but towards the end I could not deal with it anymore. It was killing me. I drank a fifth of whiskey a day. Sometimes I drank just to change it up.   One day when I lived in Fallbrook, California, I drank and blacked out as

Younger me

usual. That happened often. In fact the first time I drank, I blacked out. I never had anyone tell me about all the good things I did in a black out. There had been times that I woke up in front of judge. Most of the time I got into fights. This day was no different. I got into a fight with the people I was drinking with. Somehow I managed to drive home in a black out, then when I got home I went crazy. At the time I lived with my family – two brothers, stepfather, mother and grandmother. I staggered out of the car and started yelling and hollering at my mother. Then I started punching and beating on someone else's car. I thought the FBI was after me. I was falling down drunk and staggered over to the woodpile where my brother was and fell into it. I scraped my face up when I fell and cried out to my brother. I was crying out for help. I did not want to drink. Even in the midst of a blackout, I wanted to quit drinking. God must have heard me.

My brother and I lived upstairs in a loft in the barn and I got up there somehow. I was throwing up blood into a bucket that looked like ropes of blood. There were clots in my stomach. Then it got really bad the next morning and I started throwing up fresh blood. I drove myself to the hospital and went to the emergency room. I started throwing up again and passed out from loss of blood. I heard the nurses saying, "This one is going under." I passed out again until I woke up in the intensive care unit. By that night the bleeding had stopped. God had saved me again. The next day they put me in a regular hospital room. My mother and brother came to visit and brought some friends. I did not realize that they were part of a recovery program. A couple of days later the doctor told me I had to stop drinking or it was going to kill me. She said that next time the bleeding might not stop. With a lot of God's help and a recovery program, I stopped drinking one day at a time. As I write this, I have 29 years of no drinking, and that is a miracle, not a piece of cake. It is the best thing I have ever done, besides being saved and baptized.

That first year was a crazy time. My brother and I hung out together a lot and went to recovery places to hear how other people stayed sober. We were both crazy as a couple of loons and would drive all over the place. We were the same people, we just took away the booze. I had the shakes for a couple of weeks and crazy dreams for a couple of months. I would try to fix something on a car, but I am not good at working on cars or machines, and something would not go right. I would get so mad at the car that I'd pound on it with the tool that I had in my hand at the time. I hate to admit it but I can still get angry about little things. As I was writing this book, my other pen went out. I got angry about it, but that did not do any good. The pen still does not work. I am still learning. Sometimes I would throw my tools out in the field. I went out there to cut the grass and found a few screwdrivers and wrenches I'd thrown.

The people in the Fallbrook, California recovery program were what really helped me. In turn I get to help others. When I am feeling bad about myself or depressed, I try to find someone I can help. I don't go to the recovery place anymore. The Lord has me in a different place these days. I still work with people who have problems with alcohol and other issues. I give out sandwiches, clothing, blankets and prayer to the homeless, a hug sometimes and an ear. Sometimes I give away whatever the Holy Spirit leads me to. I thank the Lord Jesus Christ for my sobriety today. Without God in my life, I would have drunk myself to death a long time ago. We all need a spiritual foundation. One day at a time.

A LOT OF VEHICLES

A couple of years ago, a friend and I were talking about cars and trucks. He asked how many I have had, bought, sold, traded, junked, left on the side of the road or in a driveway. I did not get my drivers license until I was 26 years old because I never stayed in one place long enough. Plus, aside

from my mom's Chevette, I only ever bought one car that I kept for long. When I was traveling around the country in the carnival, I bought a big station wagon from one of my bosses that I used to get from one carnival to another and to sleep in. Some of the cars and trucks I bought, sold and traded I made a profit on, but most I lost money on. Some I was grateful to break even on. I even used one that broke down on the way home after I bought it for storing my flea market items in – now that's redneck there. I have slept in a few of the cars while traveling or between places. A lot of them I used for hauling. I would put them to work. My vehicles always made me money. I would get rid of them quick. I tried to work on own vehicles but I am not that handy with a wrench. If I think I can save a buck, I will try. On quite a few vehicles I had there were dents on the dashboard from me getting mad. I got so mad one time that I broke the steering wheel on my truck. That was a money pit of a truck, where just everything broke or cracked. As soon as I paid it off I sold it and broke even on that deal.

I bought some of the vehicles at used car dealers. I have had lemons, junkers and clunkers. One of the trucks I had caught fire. I had a '69 Cadillac that blew the engine. One junker truck I used for hauling salvage and flea market stuff. Every couple of days that truck would break down. It broke down at the wrong time one day and I got so mad that I picked up a 2x4 out of the back and started beating on it. I think I had a meltdown. A woman I knew from the recovery program was watching from upstairs. I think her jaw dropped open. She could not believe what I was doing to the truck. She stayed away from me and did not talk to me for about two years. It is amazing that I have had 40 different vehicles over the course of my life. Some vehicles were blessings, some were free and some were a curse, and those I couldn't wait to get rid of. I have dreams about the old vehicles I've bought and sold. They're all up on blocks and I am trying to fix and sell them. I still dream about the taxi driving business, too.

MANY PLACES, NO HOME

I have lived in many different places and a lot of crazy places. What does that say about me? By the time I was 20 years old, I had seen 35 states, some more than once. A lot states and cities I just passed through and did not even stop. It is amazing how many residences I have had and how many times I have moved. I lived in 43 different places from the time I was 18 years old until I got sober at 26. Since that time, I've been in another 55. It is mind boggling when I think that I have had 98 different residences. It is no wonder my own mother called me a vagabond. I have lived with roommates, family members, girlfriends and wingnuts. I lived with one woman who paid my rent, food and bought me nice things. Yes, she was older – I guess they call that being a gigolo. I have stayed in trailers, mobile homes, on people's couches and floors, in abandoned houses and construction sites. I even slept in a storage container. I have owned a trailer, lived in fancy apartments and in some places with no heat or water. I have lived in campers, cars and trucks. I've used the floor of my van and a few times I slept in my friend's van in front of his house. There have been a lot of motel and hotel rooms, some weekly places with rats and roaches and some top of the line. I have lived in a lot of campgrounds and other places in tents, and camped out in the weeds, under trees, in the bushes and

at rest areas. I have slept in -20 below weather. I camped out one night in Rabbit Ears Pass, Colorado. It was 12,000 feet in elevation. I woke up with ice on my sleeping bag and it was July. I've slept under bridges, even in a tunnel one night with a bed sheet, in parks, beaches and on the streets, never in a boat or plane though. I have stayed in a lot recovery homes and in a recovery meeting hall for a while. I've lived at missions, Salvation Armies all over the country, bunkhouses, the YMCA, and slept in many boxcars, fields and snow shelters.

As many times as I have moved or left town, I still feel like a gypsy, hobo, a vagabond. My old road name used to be Nomad, a traveling nobody. Everyone had a street name or a road name like Snake, Spider, Tiny, Tramp, Tumbleweed or Freight Train. One time my own mother called me a carpetbagger. I love my mother, but she will let you know what is on her mind. I have a funny story about the two of us. I was living with my brother in a mobile home up in Kalispell, Montana. Mom came over to visit and I was doing the dishes, grumbling and complaining about it. I told her, "You know I am going to throw these dishes out in the yard and use them for target practice. I will shoot them so I won't have to wash them again." I was serious, too. She said, "You know they have medications for people like you." I told my friend about it and she never let me forget. She'd say, "Even your own mother told you that you need medication." You know Jesus Christ was mobile and traveling for three years. I bet there were a lot of times that Jesus said, "Fox have holes and birds of the air have nests but the Son of Man has no place to lay his head."

SO MANY JOBS

I think my first working days started when I was seven or eight years old. I would go around the neighborhood with my little red wagon and collect soda bottles. Back then bottles were worth five cents each. Coca-Cola, Pepsi and RC Cola were big. I never saved anything either, just spent it. I also worked for my dad, or I tried to, in the wood business. My parents were not savers. We always had food and a roof over my head though, so I just never thought about money. My parents always gave me an allowance, $25 a week. That was a lot more than the other kids were earning. I had to work for it. I don't know why, but I hated to work. I think I was lazy and just hated to bust my back like that. For that $25 I would cut the grass and trim it, wash the car, and watch my brothers for a couple hours in the afternoon five days a week. Sometimes I would lock my brothers in their room or my friends would come over and we would smoke dope. The more dope I smoked the lazier I got. My first real job was at Der Wienersnitzel. The boss had me digging holes and pulling weeds. After two days of backbreaking work out in the hot California sun, I quit on him. I told my dad and I thought he was going to kill me he was so pissed. He was never physically abusive, but he was verbally abusive.

When I was 12, I started doing drugs and drinking. I found out I could sell drugs instead of working. It was easy money but I never made a lot. Most of my profits went to weed, alcohol and other stuff. I also found out I could steal money and rip off the dealers, which was not smart in a small town. I guess I just never got it back then. Everyone else was going to college or a trade school and getting a job. I graduated to being a beach bum. I learned how to beg people for food and money. If you had a dog it was even better because people felt for you and the dog. I had a dog when I first started bumming around that I got from an old hippie place called Hippie Hill. It was on a dirt road into the hills, with all these buses, tents,

cars, trucks and makeshift cabins. The dog was named Max, an Australian Shepard and lab mix. He was a good dog and smart. I lost him when someone stole him in Santa Barbara, California.

I found out over the years of being on the streets and all over the country that I was very good at panhandling. I also found out that I could sell my blood plasma for $20 to $30 a week. I picked cans and bottles once in a while when there were big holiday celebrations or parades. I found all the places we could eat at for free, different towns we could stop at once a month. We all got food stamps and sometimes I would cash them in and buy a little candy to get the change back. Traveling with the carnival working as an announcer and making sales was one big party. We made so much money and spent it like rock stars.

I have sold women's shoes, purses, watches, dolls, stereos, TV's, appliances, tools and golf clubs. I have bought and sold cars, trucks, motorcycles, bicycles and trailers and also sold them to salvage yards. Over the years I have sold a boatload of stuff at flea markets, yard sales and on Ebay. I have unloaded items at the market when I did not even know what they were. I was on such a roll one day at the flea market that I sold my car, too. My stepfather Curt teased me about that one. I have sold antiques to dealers and to the public. I have sold pens and pencils on the street, balloons in Portland, Oregon and Chinese yoyos in Miami, Florida, and items out of the newspaper. I drove for a couple of airport shuttle companies and about ten different taxi companies in Sacramento, California. I even drove a tourist company van in Columbia Falls, Montana. I almost drove a limo a couple times, but I chickened out.

I started a lot of different businesses over the years. I had three hauling businesses, five salvage businesses and six different flea market sales businesses. I had some ups and downs in the flea market business. One day I made $2. I was pissed that day. Then there was one day I sold $1200 worth of items. I was happy that day. I bought, sold and traded almost anything of value. I had a roofing business and a handy man business. I had a pressure washing and window cleaning business. I have even dug in dumpsters and trashcans looking for cans and bottles and stuff to sell at yard sales. I have been known to sell junk I found for $100, trash into cash. I worked as a bus boy, a dishwasher at Denny's and at Taco Bell as a fry cook. I did not eat Mexican food after that for a couple years. I was a driver for Hertz Rental Car at the airport. I also drove cars, trucks and limos at an auction company in Sacramento. I worked in pipe yards. I have unloaded and loaded trucks and boxcars. I worked for Labor Ready in a lot of places all over the country. I worked at a Christmas tree farm in Montana and was a maintenance man for a hotel there. I worked on a farm for a couple weeks. I have sold campers shells. I have cleaned pools. I sold avocados and oranges and even a big jar of peanut butter. The day after I sold it, they had a big recall on some brands of peanut butter. I was a little scared.

The Life & Times of the Rich Hobo

The Life & Times of the Rich Hobo

I have been stressed out in the hauling business. One time I got so tired of it that something set me off. I got so angry I threw everything in the truck and took it to the dump. In my fit of rage I threw all my tools and some other things away, took the hammer to racks and tore them off of the truck. I went back home and told my girlfriend about it. She said she was lucky she didn't go with me because I would probably have left her there, too. Another time, my brother and my friend Alfred and I were doing a hauling job in Fallbrook, California. We were at a job that was a money pit. We had dumpsters, a 26-foot truck and four hauling trucks. The last part of the job we were hauling sagebrush off the side of the hills. We had a makeshift road so we could load the trucks. I was backing up the 26-foot truck when the back wheel slid into the dirt on the side of the hill. The truck, which was a rental, was sinking fast. If we did not do something quick it was going to roll down the hill. I was stressing, yelling and scared. They put rock, branches and dirt under the tire. I hit the gas and said a prayer. My heart was pounding and I was sweating. Rocks and sticks were flying but I was out of the ditch and the truck was on level ground again. What a relief. It was by the grace of God I did not roll down the hill.

I have been a man of many hats, too many probably. It makes my head spin to think about it. It's a wonder I don't need pills. Maybe I do, I just don't believe in taking meds. I have also been injured quite a few times

The Life & Times of the Rich Hobo

on different jobs. It's a wonder I am still alive and walking around to tell about it. I have to admit that sometimes I have to use a cane to walk. I have fallen twice off of ladders. My feet tingle sometimes and hurt all the time. My knees hurt and sometimes my neck. I hurt my back a couple times and it cramps up. I have hurt my shoulder, pulled a muscle in my ribs and in my right arm. I even had a rattlesnake try to bite me. I chopped it in half. It still came after me and I had to chop its head off. I have been bitten twice by black widows. I have had three nervous breakdowns. I have had bouts of depression from not working and not knowing what I wanted to do with my life.

From the time I was 18 years old until now that I'm in my mid-50's, I have had over 100 different businesses and jobs. Through all of the ups and downs throughout the years, the Lord has taken very good care of me. Plus I am very fugal with what God has given me. If I get $100 on a job, I give the Lord $10 and try to give away $5 or $10. Maybe spend $10 on my-self and bank the rest. I have always been that way. Ask anyone that knows me, I hate spending money. Many times, I quit or left or messed up or got fired from jobs, and have lost many opportunities. I sold my stocks in Exxon Mobile and some other stocks. I could have been multi-millionaire a couple of times over. I realize I am a blessed man today, in spite of every-thing. That's why they call me the rich hobo.

SCENIC VIEW IN A BOXCAR

I was traveling through Montana with a friend. I had come from Florida, just to see how long it would take to hitchhike across the country from Florida to Washington. It started snowing and did not stop. All the freeways were closed. In Missoula, Montana we decided to catch a freight train to Seattle. We had to wait out at the end of the train yard where it would be pulling out slow enough for us to hop on. We would run alongside the train, throw

our gear on and then hop on the boxcar or whatever else was available. I have ridden flat cars with a trailer on them so I could hide behind the tires from the wind and the railroad police. Or we rode in grain cars, oil tankers and rail cars that hold cars. Boxcars were the best for traveling. It was still snowing like crazy and in the 20's. We were prepared for weather like that. We had to be or we would have frozen to death. We started heading into the mountains and the higher up we went, the colder it got. I did not have any gloves so I wore 2 pairs of socks on my hands to keep them from freezing. With the wind blowing on us it was more like -10 below. The view of snow covered mountains and pine trees was breathtaking. Then we went up through the passes into Washington and more beautiful scenery. It seemed to be a good time in my life. At least that day it was. Next day we might be in jail or in danger of getting shot, beat up, stabbed or beating someone else up.

There was a long tunnel that the train had to pass through. It took about 10 minutes to get through and that is a long time to be in the dark. The rule is, while you're going through the tunnel, you don't move. If you do, put a bandana over your face so you don't breathe the diesel smoke. It will kill you if you are too close to the engine. That is why you try to get a boxcar close to the back of the freight train. On this trip we were all smoking weed. We were pretty stoned. That was just part of any day. One of the hobos riding with us had a little puppy with him. I don't know if the puppy got away or the guy forgot to tie him up. When we got to the end of tunnel, we saw the light of day again. The puppy was gone. We all knew what had happened. No one said a word or talked for a long time. We all made Seattle, Washington. That was a journey I will never forget. It took me seven days to travel from Florida to Seattle. I know on every journey each time I traveled that the Lord was watching over me.

MY NEW FRIEND

I had been traveling around the country. One night I stopped for the day in a small town. It looked like a ghost town. There were no people and the buildings were all abandoned. So I rolled my sleeping bag out on the sidewalk. It was a little cold that night, in the 40's. I was so used to sleeping outside as long as I had a sleeping bag. I could not do that anymore. All of sudden a big German Shepard dog showed up. Amazingly enough, the dog laid down next to me. I let him stay the night with me. I never petted him, just let him sleep there. Maybe he was homeless, too. Maybe we kept each other warm. Maybe God sent me a protector for the night. I will never know. When I woke up the next morning, he was gone. God will always bring people into our life to help us, sometimes even animals. The Lord works in mysterious way. His ways are not our ways.

NO BATHING

One of the things about living on the streets that I don't like is the lack of bathing and clean clothing. I have smelled so bad that one time that one time it was like a cattle truck. Another time in Kalispell, my friend Jack got me a room at the Kalispell Grand Hotel. The bed was so nice I didn't want to get it dirty. The room had a big shower and a big screen TV. I lived at a Howard Johnson's in Florida for two weeks on vacation. It was a four-star hotel. After living on the streets, I really get spoiled in a motel with a shower every night. Sometimes I shower three or four times a day. Sometimes I would just get a motel for a night, especially around the tourist season. I tried to get a room one time in Manhattan, Kansas. The fancy hotel did not want me renting a room in their high-end place. I think they were afraid that I would come out of the room in my thermal underwear and boots on, running around scaring the guests. I hate to say it, but the high-end hotels don't like hobos in their establishment. Most churches are the same way. If you look homeless, they treat you differently than if you were all dressed up. People, churches, restaurants, hotels all treat you differently. I have even done that before myself. I have to take the pole out of my own eye, too. I am dressed up as I write this so I can get a job at the

Burger King in Kalispell, Montana.

TRAVELING

When the road calls, you've got to go. It is a yearning that gets in your soul. Trains, planes and automobiles, just like the movie. You get tired of one place so you go to another place and visit, then you're down the road again. I have traveled a lot this year of 2015. I left Manhattan, Kansas and got on the train in Topeka. I went to Chicago, then Washington DC, then to Jacksonville and St. Augustine Florida. After a few weeks, I got back on the train and went all the way to Whitefish, Montana. I was questioning my sanity traveling in the wintertime, going from Florida where it was 65 degrees, to Montana where it was snowing and a lot colder. The cold weather is especially bad if you are living on the streets. Most people don't wear as many clothes as homeless people do. We are out in it, we have to dress in layers. I like to be warm but sometimes I have too many layers. The coldest I've slept out in the weather was in my Buick at 10 below. Now that is cold.

I have traveled in every kind of weather you can think of, and by every means possible. I've hitchhiked, walked, ridden freight trains, airplanes, the Amtrak and driven my own vehicles. I have been stranded in towns, on freeways, roadsides, snow banks, been snowed in and run off by the police. I've left town because it was time to go and the road was calling. Some days when the sun is out and it's springtime, you look at the day and say it would be great to get the hell out of here. I always say, lighten your load and hit the road. Go somewhere new, make new friends and unfortunately, new enemies. There are always some people who will piss you off. That's why I leave some places, too many people start pissing me off. It becomes time to go and get away from them and sometimes I never go back. Sometimes I can't go back because of the police.

My bucket list is to see all the United States, then see Australia and maybe some other countries. Go on a safari in Africa, go to Bethlehem where Jesus was born and Galilee where He walked. Maybe go to Tokyo and Hong Kong, take a cruise ship around the world. I love to travel and don't think I'll ever settle down until I am in Heaven. Then I will rest. I seem to have a restless spirit. Some birds you cannot cage. That is the way the Lord made me, I am not going to apologize for it. I am living the dream and I am rich in the Lord and my life, even with all the aches and pains. That's when I trust in the Lord even more, one day at a time.

CRAZINESS IN BUSINESS

I have done so many crazy things in my business life. There has been a lot of blood, sweat and tears, stress, anxiety, even medications a few times, court appearances, lawsuits. In the old days I drank a lot of beer and whiskey. If I had all the money back that I drank up, I could be a millionaire. I had a yard sale where I made nothing and another day I made $1200 at the flea market. One day I made $3,200 in my hauling business. I have been broke so many times it would make your head spin, but usually not for

long. There have also been many times when I have made money out of nothing. Remember I said broke, not poor. Broke is temporary. Also, I have been injured so many times on different jobs, sometimes I felt like I was riding in a rodeo. I know today God saved me many times on jobs. One time I fell off of a ladder about 10 feet up. I was cutting a tree limb down off the fence. The limb shifted when I was cutting it, the ladder moved and down I went. Lucky I dropped the chainsaw before I fell. I landed on my feet and thought I was ok. Picked up the chainsaw, started back to work and finished the job. The next day I could not get out of bed. The following day, the chiropractor said my back looked and felt like a pile of rocks. My legs, especially my calves were cramping up badly, my back and neck, too. My friend Eric gave me a key to the Jacuzzi. I used that hot tub with the jets massaging the muscles in my calves for about a month. It took me about two months to get back to 100% physically. When I fell, God was watching out for me. I landed on a pile of leaves and a few small limbs. On the right side of me was a metal pipe sticking out of the ground. To the left of me was a tree. Behind me was a concrete walkway.

I guess I have never been rich or wealthy. The most I ever made in one year was $25,000 profit. There have been years when I have only made $3,500. That is poverty. God has given me a gift of being frugal, not spending unless I absolutely have to. I also have to find deals on housing. God always provides a place. Sometimes I house sit for people. I have worked for room and board. There have been other times I had to sleep on a couch outside. It was ok, believe it or not. I buy stuff I want, always at a discount – or free is even better. I buy stuff knowing one day I might sell if for a profit. I had some friends give me a gift on my birthday. They told me I could not sell it. They know me too well. I used it for a while, then turned around and sold it, I hate to say. They still tell me not to sell my gifts. I feel like I am broke unless I have a wad of cash in my pocket. I have never been a hoarder of things. You can't make a profit from keeping things. That's why my stepfather said he would never give me anything when he dies. He said you'll just sell it. He's probably right. I also found out about tithing since I have been a Christian. No matter how much money I make, if it is $1 or $10,000, I give 10% of my gross, not my net. God said he wanted the first fruits. I try to give another 10% to the homeless, widows and orphans. That is why I am never broke. I always have money in the bank and in my pocket. That's why I call myself the rich hobo. Some people say I can't afford to do that, but you can't afford not to.

I have started over so many times in business. I say I starting with nothing and pretty much have most of it left. That's funny. I have come from nothing and made something out of it. I fell off another ladder doing some painting. I reached too far and the ladder fell one way and I fell the other way. I was done with that painting job. That was in September, then in December I strained the muscles in my back and neck. I pulled a groin muscle, tweaked my right shoulder, all from the fall and also I was pushing a van by myself out of the street. I had so many things going wrong in my body. I was in so much pain. I was used to pain; it was nothing new. I was hurting so bad I applied for disability. On top of everything I was depressed. I could not work. I had no income and a van that needed work. I was living behind the church.

I knew from past sales and panhandling experience that people are very generous around Christmas time with their money, especially if you are out there trying to make a sale. I started this venture with $131 in my pocket. I went to the Dollar Tree and bought some pens and pencils, scotch tape and paper. I wrote little Christmas notes, inspirational notes and Christian quotes. I taped them on the pens and pencils. I put the pencils and pens in a glass coffee mug and a sign on the mug saying, "50 cents each or 3 for $1, Thank You." The first place I went was to an off ramp. In the first five minutes a lady pulled up in a big Cadillac Escalade and gave me a twenty-dollar bill. I was surprised. The highway patrol told me to get off the off ramp. Then I made another $2. Someone called the police on me. They told me I had to have a business license to sell pens and pencils. So I changed my sign to, "Disabled, I can't work and need a little help, Free pen or pencil." It sounds like an easy way to make money. It is not. The looks and scowls you get. I did not know what was colder, the weather or the people.

It was so painful sometimes. My back would cramp up, then my legs would. Then my feet hurt so badly from standing. I brought a bucket with me so I could sit down. Being overweight did not help any. I could only stand out there about three hours, then I would start falling apart. It was amazing, some days I made $25, some days I made $90 for three hours. I got run off from more off ramps and corners. I even got a ticket one time. It was only by the grace of God that I made $1,300 for that Christmas season. I did the same thing the next year. I sold pens and pencils with candy canes on them. Then I guess I crossed over into panhandling. I went from making $25 to $50 a day, to $60, to $135 a day. That can get kind of addicting. Easy money. I have also sold flower pens on Valentine's Day and Mother's Day.

Most of the time when I buy cars, trucks, bicycles or anything I can use, I know that I am going to sell it, later or right away. Sometimes I tear stuff up, too. Sometimes I can't sell it and make a profit. One time in Fallbrook, I started a hauling business with a little Ford Courier and $100 in the bank. I was in recovery. I had a lot of help from others, too, like my girlfriend Teresa although she won't admit it. We had a lot of fun. She bought me a penny saver ad for a month. She let me dump some vegetation and limbs. She gave me a truckload of cans on time. She liked helping me. My mother let me store my trucks, and piles of stuff and a dumpster. My brother Ralph helped me a lot. An artist friend of mine drew me up a logo for little or nothing. My stepfather sold me the truck. I had a lot of help from God. That year I grossed $48,000, too bad that was not the net, which was zero. I started a business pressure washing and window cleaning on a bicycle. Then I got a truck and had more business than I could handle. I have done so many different things in my life, it makes my head spin. All I can say is, Wow. I have lost and spent a million dollars. This next million dollars, I am going to save as much as I can, invest as much as I can, give away as much as I can. I would give to God's Kingdom. He will always take care of you. Plant seed in someone else's life. See what God will do.

THE HUSTLER

I don't like being called a hustler. I have been called that quite a few times. One time I was living in a house in Ranch Cordova, California with a lot of roommates. Seems like my whole life I have had some kind of roommates, family and friends. Being a roommate will test any friendship. I've had girlfriends for roommates and have lived on my own a few times. In this particular house I lived in, one guy was from India. He was something else. He was a crook and left a trail of deception a mile long. He was the kind of person that would talk you out of your stuff or he would steal it, then try to sell it back to you. We did a few deals together. I was kind of ruthless back then myself. I am not proud of that. That was just the way I was back then. One time we both went to the Folsom flea market. We had a contest to see who was the better hustler. We both had twenty dollars each. We had to buy and sell at the flea market and whoever came up with the most profit from the $20 won. We looked around and I finally found a leather jacket for $40. I haggled with the seller and got the jacket for $20. Then about five minutes later I sold it to another dealer for $35. I won the contest. Not bad for five minute's worth of haggling. I bought a car from one of my East Indian roommate's friends. Come to find out the car would not start. I think I bought it for $100. I never could get it running so I sold it as is for $150. I signed and they towed it away. That was amazing to sell a car that did not even run. Then he went to India and left me a walnut dining room set to sell. I sanded the chairs and shined them up. They were antiques. I borrowed someone's truck and took the set to the flea market. I had barely unloaded when I sold it to a dealer for $250. This was back in 1991. He probably turned around and sold it for $500 to $750 or more, plus I sold some other items that day. I made $300 altogether, a very profitable day. It beats the heck out of working all day.

Another time I went to a different flea market. It was called the 49er Drive In. Anyone that sold anything in Sacramento knew the 49er. My friend Jeff and I were late one day. Back then I hated getting up early. I had a little Dodge Colt so I could park anywhere and I found a spot. We unloaded the car but didn't have a table. I had a lot of miscellaneous odd and ends, a little bit of everything. I just threw it on the ground to sell near all these spaces with people that had big tables of glassware and all kinds of nice stuff. I was right in the middle of it and sold everything in about an hour's time. I made $35 while those other people were not selling anything. My friend was amazed that I was able to sell a bunch of junk on the ground so fast. Another time I bought two bins full of golf clubs and bags for $25 for all of them. I turned around and made $700 off of them. I also took the irons that would not sell to the salvage yard for the price I paid for them. I used to buy bins of junk. There was some good stuff in there sometimes – tools, antiques, records, a lot of household stuff. I hated the dishes and glassware. We would bid on the bins full of junk and get them for $30 to $50, then take it out to the flea market and try to get $100 to

$150 for it all. Some days were $75 or $80.

I always seemed to make a profit, just enough for food, gas and cigars. Never had enough for car breakdowns, rent or luxuries. Some of the people really pissed me off. I would get so fed up with loading and unloading all that junk, I would sell it for almost nothing just to get rid of it. So I could do it all again. There were quite a few times when I sold all I had and would go look for other people's stuff they did not want anymore. If a dealer wanted to sell out so he could buy some more, we would haggle over a price. It was usually $10 or $20 for everything, then I would make $20 or $30 profit selling out to another dealer. I would make $70 to $80 just hustling at the flea market sales. Flea markets have changed a lot now. They are too high in table rent, permits, sales license, less time. Another time I was at the flea market and I wanted to go home so I yelled out, "Everything is free but donations are welcome." I could not believe it, I made $20 just off of donations. Selling at the flea market with people buying and haggling, you come home with a pocket full of money and I love days like that. Whoever said money doesn't make you happy, never had any. It reminds me of the carnival days. I still have a little bit of carny and hobo in me. When I have a big sale or count up my money at the end of a job or money I have saved up, I say to myself, not bad for an old carny and hobo. My friend Daniel called me a rich hobo. It stuck and I considered it a compliment. I tried to tell him I was going broke and he told me to just check my other pocket.

God has given me a gift to turn trash into cash. I know how to make nothing into something. One man's junk is another man's treasure. One of my great uncles was like that. My mother told stories about him wheeling and dealing and trading. My grandfather was the same way. He was known to be a great salesman. God gives each one of us a gift. It is up to us if we use that gift or not. We are already blessed, we just have to reach out and ask God for wisdom. It is like the story of the man who had a farm and was barely making it, but he had big dreams of being rich. Someone told him about the riches of diamonds, so he sold the farm for pennies on the dollar. He traveled all over the world, looking, digging and exploring for diamonds. After years of looking, he was dressed in rags and died broke. Years later, the guy who bought the farm found a stone and put it on the fireplace mantel. His friend came over one night and asked where he got the stone. He said, "I found it a couple of months ago. I thought the stone looked nice so I put it on the mantle." His friend said, "That is no stone, that is a diamond." It was the biggest diamond he had ever seen. The farm turned out to be the world's largest diamond mine, and the whole time the original farmer had acres of diamonds right in his own backyard. That is just like the story about the guy who buys a junkyard and later finds out he had the biggest deposit of oil in the country right under his house and land. He did not know about it until a geologist did some tests and told him there was oil in the ground. The junk dealer was barely getting by until he tapped into the gusher of oil and then he was a very rich man.

That is the way God wants us to live – rich, wealthy, with more than enough. Overflowing. Sad to say, but most of us don't live that way. A lot of us live and barely get by mentally. God does not want his children to live that way. He wants to bless you big time. We have to ask and have faith. Believe it and you will receive it.

THE BULLETS

My East Indian roommate was leaving for India. He said to me that he wanted to sneak some bullets into his country. He though he had a brilliant idea. He was going to melt some plastic around the bullets. He put them in the oven. The oven heated the bullets up. They started going off, sounding like firecrackers exploding. They were firing off in the oven. A few shot into the cabinet, a few shot into the counter and floor. Wow, lucky no one was in the kitchen. He found out that bullets and oven heat don't mix.

EL PASO, TEXAS

A bunch of us were riding around on the train. We always rode in groups because it was safer in larger numbers and it was dangerous riding the trains. We were all down in El Paso, Texas. We had been drinking and smoking weed that night. I blacked out again. I think everyone else did, too. We all woke up on the train in a coal car. There was no coal in the car, but a lot of coal dust. We had coal dust all over our clothes and our sleeping bags and all over our faces. It was funny. All you could see was the whites of our eyes and our teeth. We did not look white anymore; we were all black men and just started laughing.

ANGRY

I have had a temper for a long time. I think I came out of the womb mad. When the doctor smacked me, I got angry at him. I have gotten a lot better than in the old days. I can remember one time when I first was in recovery I had another brilliant idea. I thought I was going to fix the lawn mower. I started on it and I could feel my blood pressure rising. I fixed the lawn mower all right. I fixed it with a hammer. I started smashing and I could not stop. Pieces and parts were flying. I was sweating and shaking. I had no business trying to fix a lawn mower with my patience. I don't even like

mechanic work. I went into a rage that day. I still get angry, but I look at it like what would Jesus do and I don't go into those rages anymore. I also dealt with a lot of my issues – resentments, hatred, prejudice and unforgiveness when I was in recovery. I made a list of people that had done me wrong, people I was angry at. It helped a lot. The Lord has taught me to forgive others and especially my enemies. I have gotten into so much trouble over my anger. I have lost more women, jobs, business opportunities and friendships. I usually have friends that are angry, too, or they run the other way. I have had contracts in my businesses where I did the job with pure anger or would get so frustrated at the end of the job, they would not have me come back. I have been fired from so many jobs or I would get so angry I would quit. Yes, anger has taken its toll on me. I am not proud of this or bragging about it. When I get angry I clench my teeth together. I have teeth that are cracked, chipped and gone from grinding them together. I have had ulcers and high pressure. One time I started arguing with someone over the phone and I got so mad I started having pains in my heart area. I have gone to jail because of beating someone up. I have gotten fined, into arguments, conflicts and even fights. Twice in the cab business, I punched the windshield. In that business, people really made me angry. That is why I did not carry a gun – I would have shot someone or I would have shot out streetlights. I did not like red lights, that is why I drove the taxi at night in less traffic. A lady wanted to sue the cab company because of me. I also got fired from the best company I ever worked for. They bent over backwards to help me and paid me well, too. I had too many complaints that I had gotten mad at animals. I used to have regrets about everything I lost over anger. I can't live in regret, all I can do is just choose not to be angry today. Deal with things so that I am not angry about one thing when really I am angry about something else. It is my choice to be happy or angry. I know I still have a long ways to go. I am not perfect. Jesus was the only perfect man that lived on Earth. Thank God for his grace, He forgives us. I have to remember to forgive myself.

THE GIANT

One time I was driving a taxicab for Yellow Cab Company in Sacramento, California. I was driving at night in the north area of the city. Things could get crazy in the north area sometimes, and crazy downtown, too. So I was called on the radio to pick up at a certain address. I went to the door and knocked, and when the door opened I saw that the people there were drunk. A guy and his wife came outside and said, "Take this guy downtown. We will give you the $20 taxi fare and a $5 tip." This guy comes out of the house who is so tall that he has to duck under the door to get out. He hooted, hollered and was carrying on. They wanted him out of there. I couldn't blame them, he was about 6' 5" and weighed about 400 pounds. This guy was a giant, his arms looked like my legs. His legs looked like tree trunks. He had long hair and tattoos all over him. He was scary. I did not let him know that; you show no fear in the cab business. I learned that living on the streets and from traveling around. Show your fear in those places and you will be in trouble. The people that paid said he had just gotten out of prison. He could have joined with WWF as a wrestler. He got into the cab and so did I. I felt so little compared to him. I am 5'6" and 175 pounds. He was so big I almost did not have enough room to drive. He was clapping his hands together and talking crazy. The smart thing for me to do was just agree with everything he said. I am sure glad he did not try to pick a fight with me. He would have crushed me with one hand. I still couldn't believe how big this guy was. I think he had 28 or 30-inch arms. I finally dropped him off downtown. I was happy to get him out of the cab. I was still alive and in one piece. That is the way we look at our problems, like giants. Our God is bigger than those giants.

THE MONTANA SURVIVOR

I moved from West Sacramento, California to Columbia Falls, Montana. I drove up there with a little car that I bought for $100. I stayed with my brother at the campground in a tent. He lived in an overhead camper. He took it off the truck he lived in, then after a couple days I started sleeping in the camper on a makeshift mattress. I loved it. It was at the campground with beautiful scenery. I toured around the place for a couple of days then started looking for work. I worked with my brother; he had a handyman business. I looked at temp places for work. I saw a deal one day at the store parking lot. It was a 71 Chevrolet pick up with an overhead camper so I bought it for $1,000. I think he wanted $1,500. I got another deal, love it. I sold the car for $490 and lived in the camper for eight months. I used the truck to haul stuff. It was the coldest winter they had in years. It was bone chilling cold. I had to walk to the shower and the bathroom in the morning. I survived it, then my brother sold me his car for $300. So I sold my truck to my stepfather for a $1,000. Then we had to move from the campground. My brother and I both had to tear down the camper. We could not sell them in the condition they were in so I tore mine

The Life & Times of the Rich Hobo

down and hauled all the scrap and wood to the dump. I used the car. I am always turning my cars into trucks, not good. We moved into a motel for a month. Wow, was that an experience and noisy. I got a job working at a motel in Whitefish. I was a man of many hats. That is the way I liked it and I fit right in. I got along with everyone there. I was the maintenance man and did room service and the airport shuttle drive. I would drive to Costco to do the shopping for breakfast. I set up and tore down for banquets, I made the coffee, checked the pools and I drove people to dinner. I did the gardening, put salt on the ice in the wintertime and painted touchup in the rooms. My schedule was 3pm to 11pm. I loved it most of the time.

During the day sometimes I would sell items. I would go to the thrift store on Thursday. It was only open one day a week. I bought their army gear and hunting jackets for a couple dollars each, sometimes a dollar. Then Friday or sometimes that same day, I would sell the stuff to the Army Navy store, for $10 or $20 sometimes. Sometimes I would only get $5, then would buy Christian CD's and tapes. I would sell them to the Christian bookstore. I would go to the dump because they let you scrounge around in there. Everything I found at the dump, I would take to the consignment shop once a month and get a check. Sometimes I would buy and sell items, tools and miscellaneous junk to the pawnshops. I made $40 off of a mower I found at the dump. I would make tips driving the shuttle. I had it made until I lifted up a toilet the night before I was supposed to leave for another shuttle company. That is what I really wanted to do – drive a shuttle. I did not like the maintenance part of it. I hated it most of the time. That night I pulled a muscle in my back. I don't know why I did not let them know right away and waited for a couple days. I went to work for the shuttle company. I could not handle all the sitting and luggage handling and I told the boss that. I went through my savings account. It is a horrible feeling when you put your ATM card in to get $20 out and you don't have enough. I think I had $12 to my name and my rent was due. That's a bad feeling, too. It was just a matter of time before they gave me a 30-day notice.

I still had my car, so I was selling a few items that I found at the dump. Plus I cashed in some cans and bottles. I could only do so much. I was still in pain from my back injury and was taking pain medications. I sold a lot of stuff so I would not have so much to move, then my car broke down I had to sell it to the junk yard for $75. So I moved in with my brother. Workers Comp was fighting me. I was seeing doctors, but nothing was helping the pain. They agreed that they were going to pay medical bills but not for my time off. So there I was at my brother's house. He had just gotten an older mobile home. I don't think he charged me any rent. It was November. I had no money. I could not work very much, if any. Most of the time when my brother hired me for a painting job it was easy work, but it took me forever it was so painful. I think he helped me on another job. I picked up something out of the truck and felt a flash of lightening up my back, down I went and crawled to the seat of the truck. He took me home. Oh my God, every bump he hit caused so much pain. I did not want to do any more physical work after that. Truth is, no matter what I did or did not do I was always in pain, especially in the cold weather in Montana.

By December 1st the snow was coming down. I had $70 to my name. I was in pain, there were no buses and I had no car. I did not know what I was going to do. I remembered from years past when I was on the streets that people are very generous with their money around Christmas time. So I found some cardboard and wrote on it, Hurt my back, waiting on SSD so I am selling Christmas pencils and pens .50 cents each or 3 for $1. I put little sayings on Christmas notes on the pens and pencils. I sold them for about three hours a day, sometimes two hours. I made about $300 over about 10 days worth of selling. One time I fell on the ice and sprained my finger. I did not have the money for a doctor so I put a popsicle stick on my finger and wrapped it up. My brother was ripping out all the paneling in the mobile home and replacing it with sheetrock. Some spots were bare, with no paneling and no insulation. It was so cold in the mobile home it was like an icebox. One night the windows froze on the inside. On January 3rd I started getting sick. I got a cold then I got the flu, then the cold went down into my chest and I got bronchitis, then I was bad. The way the mobile home was, I am surprised I did not get pneumonia.

My friend called me. She heard my situation and sent me a train ticket the next day. No point in staying – it was cold all the time with no vehicle, no buses, no jobs and my body hurt all the time. I could not get to my recovery meetings and I could not get to church. I was ready to go crazy or have a drink or both. I knew it was time to go the night before I left. My brother and I were in the van and it was -45 below that night. I have been in a lot of cold places, but it was so cold that night, when we broke down in the van we could not go outside. My brother called a friend of his and he came and picked us up in his vehicle. That was the longest half hour.

When I got back home, I had to thaw out my feet. The night I left on the train from Whitefish. It was -20 below and when I got off the train in Sacramento it was 55 degrees. What a difference. Jesus will be with us in the storm. He will calm the storm. Why are you so stressed ye of so little faith.

FRIENDS ON THE STREET

I have made some really great friends on the streets and also met some people I really didn't like. When you are living on the streets or on the road traveling to all kinds of cities and towns, you meet a lot of different people. I have friends in Sacramento, California named Kim and Allen Dee, who are really nice people. They blessed me when I lived there with work, money and their friendship. My other friends Bill and Kathy used to let me use their car. Bill and I went to breakfast at McDonald's often. Then there are John, Pam and Joy, who are good people. John helped me a lot and let me stay in his van that was parked in front of his house. He let me work for him and loaned me the van to drive. I use to house sit there and watch the movies. Shannon and Daniel have been my friends through it all. I met them

in West Sacramento living in a little trailer. They have always had animals and people they help. They have big hearts. My best friends are Larry and Darcy. They are prayer warriors and Larry is my brother in Christ. Another of my very best friends lives in Alabama. We have

kept in touch for years and he is closer than a brother. We keep up with what's going on in each other's lives. Sometimes we call when the other one is having a melt down and we've been able to help each other.

I have met some crazy people on the streets, too. One of them slapped me one day. I said to him, "You get that one for free." I looked him right in the eye and said, "I rebuke you in the name of Jesus." I could tell he had demons in him. He stopped and looked at me. He did not slap me again and walked away. Even the demons tremble at the name of Jesus. When I had my sandwich ministry in West Sacramento, California, I met a lot of people. Some were crazy, drunk or drug addicts. Many of them were just out on the streets because of bad situations. I got to pray for people out there living on the street. I was out there myself, living in a vacant apartment.

I met some neat people in Fallbrook, California, too. I have known Alfred for years. He is still cutting and selling wood in his 70s. I have good friends in Manhattan, Kansas. I didn't know there was a Manhattan in that state until I moved there. Lee is a man in his 70s, with a dog and a van. We

have had a lot of laughs together. I also met a very nice lady there named Mell, who helped me a lot and has given me a place to stay. I think she has adopted me every time I show up. One time I left town without telling anyone because that is how I used to do it – leave town, gone, easier that way. Nowadays, everyone worries

The Life & Times of the Rich Hobo

about me. Mell said she was looking for me all over the city. She was mad and worried. When I lived in Kalispell, Montana the first time, I met some really good people. I always come back to Montana because the people are so nice. I met two women, Kelly and Emili, from the Fresh Life Church who I call angels. That is what they sound like when they are singing.

Good friends are hard to come by when you are tramping around the country. Street friends are different. You never know if you are ever going to see them again. I had a friend die on the streets of Kalispell from pneumonia. Friends can die from sickness or freeze to death, go to jail or they might leave town. I told a lady in Manhattan, "Don't fall in love with us. We are a bunch of street gypsies, tramps and hobos. We might be gone, no guarantees." But I always come back to Montana because I love it here and now I have two new friends, Jessie and Guy. That still won't keep me forever though. I love to travel to new places and meet new people. I always tell my friends that I am living the dream. No one is closer than a brother who will lay down his life for you. That is what Jesus did. He laid down his life for us. He can be and should be your best friend. He will never leave you or forsake you. (Proverbs 27:17)

WINDOWS AND PRESSURE WASHING

I was working for an auction company and was not making enough money. I found out working for myself was sure a lot better. I made just as much working for myself one day as I did working for the auction company in a week. I still had a bicycle that I carried my hose, bucket, soap and brush on for  the first few jobs. I made enough to get a small 1982 Dodge D-10 truck for $400. It cost me $400 to fix it up so I could get a title for it. Sometimes I made $90 before noon. I loved it. One time I made $260 in one day for four hours worth of work. I was hooked. I did a lot of odd jobs, yard work, painting, window cleaning and then I worked for labor part time. I did a lot of hauling and salvage jobs. The first week I had the truck, the head gasket in the engine started leaking coolant. I was worried. I just spent all my money on this truck. My mechanic friend told me to put some Bar's Leaks in the radiator and it did not leak after that. I was proud of myself for about four years, I still am. I had to finally sell the truck. The economy went south and so did my business. I sold my pressure washer and tools. I don't do little odd jobs any more. God always takes care of us no matter what the economy is doing.

THE SHOOTING

I was driving taxi one night in 1995. My dispatcher radioed a call to me when I was in the downtown area. It was to a bar called The Shot of Class. I was driving down the alleyway to get to the bar when all of a sudden I saw police officers in the alley. They looked like they were ready to shoot someone. Then I heard shots fired, five or six, maybe ten shots. I saw the cops pull their pistols out and people started running all over the bar. I was scared and I did not scare easy. I put the taxi in reverse and it was like something in a movie. I got the hell out of there. I was driving in reverse about 40 miles per hour through the alley. I wanted out of there. I could have gotten shot that night. I chewed the dispatcher out that night. The dispatchers are supposed to be listening to the police scanner so they don't send a driver into a bad situation.

THE BLUFF

I was driving a cab one day and the dispatcher gave me a call. A man got into the front seat. I never did like people sitting in the front. We started making small talk. Next thing you know he pulled out this big buck knife. He started waving it around and said, "I can really cut someone up with this." He asked me, "What do you think of this knife?" I learned in the cab business being around people that it is a lot better to agree with everything they say – especially a crazy person. I said I was impressed with the knife. I told him, "I also have something under the seat. It has six shots and a pearl handle." I told him to put the knife away or he would see what I had under the seat. I bluffed him, thank God. He put the knife away. It could have gone a lot worse.

THANKSGIVING DAY MIRACLE

The Life & Times of the Rich Hobo

I have seen some miracles in my Christian walk. I was at the church for Thanksgiving. I thought I was just going to be serving the homeless dinner for Thanksgiving. There was a lot of food. God had something else in store that day. I was serving mashed potatoes. Next I knew, I was out there in the dining area talking to people who were getting gifts of some free jackets and clothes. All of a sudden the Holy Spirit hit me. I started praying for those men. I went back to the dining room. I saw a man sitting at a table. I sat down and he started telling me his story, how he had been homeless. He said he was suffering from throat cancer. Doctors only gave him so long to live and he looked like he was on his deathbed. The Lord led me to get some prayer warriors together and pray for this man's healing. I started praying for him and then this lady also started praying. We were all laying hands on him, too. I felt the Holy Spirit strongly. There was some power in that dining room. The lady was praying in Spanish. I saw the man healed right before my eyes. I saw color come back into his eyes and face. He looked like a different person. This man was healed. He hugged all of us. He knew he was healed, too. I missed church the next week after we prayed for him. Someone told me he was dancing around and jumping. He was a new person. I saw him a couple years later on the bus and he said he went to the doctor a month later. The doctor said he could not find any cancer. What a joy to be a part of that miracle.

ENEMY TO A FRIEND

I lived in West Sacramento, California for almost 17 years, so I know a lot of people there. I worked for a lady named Edith at a trailer park in exchange for rent. I would do odd jobs around her house, mostly yard work. I lived with a person named Robert. Like some of us, he use to drink. He was a happy drunk most of the time. One day I bumped his mirror with my arm, and he told me that night while he was drunk that he was going to kill anyone that was messing with his car. He started yelling. I said to myself, I don't have to put up with this. I packed up my things and the next morning I was gone. I found another place to live quick after that. I worked for a couple of little old ladies in the mobile home park. I would see him a couple of times a month. That man cost me $1,000 dollars worth of work. Every time we saw each other we wanted to get in a fight. I think we even yelled at each other a few times.

I moved to Sacramento, California and did not see him for about a year. One day out of the blue, Robert's girlfriend called me and said Robert wanted to see me – of all people. We were bitter enemies. I prayed about it. I still put it off a day or so. The Lord told me it was time to go over there and visit him. I had no idea what the Lord had in store. I started over there to his place on my bicycle. All of a sudden this swarm of bees came out of a rose bush. I thought they were going to attack me or start stinging me. There were at least 100 of them. I did not get stung one time. That was God making sure I got to my destination. When I finally got over there to visit, he was sitting on the bed. He looked yellow and like he was at death's door. He'd lost a lot of weight. First thing he said to me was, "I have been waiting for you. I want you to read me some scriptures from the Bible." He knew I was a man of God. I said, "Wait a minute. Let me lay hands on you and pray for you." I started praying and laid my hand on his shoulder. The Holy Spirit was powerful. He was in the room that day. I asked him to receive Jesus into his heart. He said the sinner's prayer. I read some more scripture, prayed some more and we both hugged each other. We both started crying and forgiving each other. All that hatred we had for each other just melted away. God surprised us that day. What a blessing that he was turning my enemy into a brother in Christ. I even prayed for his girlfriend that day, too. A couple weeks later he passed away. The angels took him home.

30 BELOW

I was traveling through Montana in the middle of winter and hooked up with another fellow hobo. It is better to travel with someone, especially on the trains or on the streets since it can be a dangerous place. Two is safer than one and it is good to have a friend. It got lonely out there on the road sometimes. We were walking one night on the streets of Missoula, Montana and it was so cold that night, probably -30 below. We found a motor home on this lot with trailers and campers. We tried the doors and finally one opened up and we were out of the weather. It was still cold in the motor home with no heat. We both realized to keep from freezing to death and keep warm, we had to bunk together in one sleeping bag. Neither one of us liked the idea but we did it anyway so we did not freeze to death. Frostbite is not a good thing to suffer from. On the same trip we caught a train out of Missoula. The next night we found a church to keep us from repeating a night in the camper again. We broke into the church and had some food compliments of the church. It was warm and we slept there all night. I know we were not supposed to break into a church. I think the Lord forgave us, we were in a time of need. What better place to be at in a time of need.

CRAZY TIMES

Throughout the years I have been dealing with anger issues, depression, anxiety and panic attacks. I have not had one in a long time. One time I was in a West Sacramento recovery meeting and I had a panic attack for the first time. I thought it was a heart attack. I could not breath right and my heart felt like it was going to pound out of my chest. My arms and body were tingling. The fire department showed up and said it was a panic attack. A day before I had the panic attack, I had a tooth pulled. They had to cut the bone in my jaw so I was in a lot of pain. I took the pain medicine for a couple days then the pain stopped, so I stopped taking the painkillers. They said that was what threw me into a panic. I realized all we have is one day at a time here on Earth. Sometimes I can still think too much and get a panic attack going. I don't do it. I ask for God's help. I breathe, calm down.

LIFE ON THE STREETS

There is a feeling on the streets that I miss sometimes. Watching the sun come up, watching the weather come in. You get to see a thunderstorm firsthand. No responsibilities, no bills. Also no place to call home. There is also a certain emptiness about not having a home. I think we humans were meant to have some kind of shelter, from the outside, from animals and from other people. We need a place to cook food, to eat, a safe place to sleep. Bathing is very important. Especially if you

have a family, you really need a place. I met a man last year who had six kids, two dogs and a cat. They were living in a motor home that they traveled around in. He had written scriptures all over the RV. They were really neat people and I meet all kinds.

There is a also a madness that comes with life on the streets, and a sadness that gets in your soul. I believe that each day you are on the streets, it takes a little piece of your soul. There is also a freedom from bills, car payments, mortgages and all the other responsibilities of life. There is freedom in living off the grid, sometimes without even a phone. You are always waiting when you live on the streets. It doesn't matter which city it is, they are all the same. You are waiting for the library to open up. Every town and city has a library to use. When you are homeless, the library is a place to get out of the cold on a winter's day or evening. Or you can get out of the heat of the summer. It is a place to read or rest. A lot of times at night when you live on the street, you don't get much sleep. Every sound wakes you up. The train comes by if you are sleeping near the railroad tracks, or there are noisy cars and trucks. Sometimes it's people partying and making noise with their car stereos. You are always worried about someone, or a bunch of people, jumping you or robbing you while you are sleeping. Hobos around the country have been stabbed or beaten with a bat while in their sleeping bags. One was even lit on fire. Some people are evil.

Then you have to worry about the other homeless stealing your stuff. Not because they need it, but just because they need to steal it seems like. A lot of times, you can't carry all your stuff around town, so we hide it in the bushes, in the trees, in the tall grass. The worst feeling in the world is when you come back to your stash place and everything has been stolen. What little bit you had is gone. Or sometimes the police will take it if you live on the street. No matter how careful you are, it will happen to you at least once. That life will bring out the crazy in you; if you're already crazy, you will be a little bit more. I think you live almost like an animal. You sleep in bushes, tents and sleeping bags by the tracks, on cardboard by the church, in cars, trucks and boxcars. Sometimes you stay wherever you can find shelter and safety. We deal with rain, thunderstorms, snow and wind. Bugs like mosquitoes are the worst. Through all these trials and tribulations, I have been able to make out on the streets. There have been a lot of times when I've gotten to help others on the streets with clothes, blankets, sleeping bags, food and money. I have helped them with prayer and guidance and led a few to the Lord. I got to preach one time and have seen healings and laid hands on others. What a blessing.

This is my mother's favorite scripture, from Psalms 27:1-5. The Lord is my light and my salvation; whom shall I fear? The Lord is the strength of my life; of whom shall I be afraid? When the wicked came against me to eat up my flesh, my enemies and foes, they stumbled and fell. Though an army may encamp against me, my heart shall not fear; though war may rise against me, in this I will be confident. One thing I have desired of the Lord, that will I seek: that I may dwell in the house of the Lord all the days of my life, to behold the beauty of the Lord, and to inquire in His temple. For in the time of trouble He shall hide me in His pavilion; in the secret place of His tabernacle He shall hide me; He shall set me high upon a rock.

BLESSED ONE DAY AT A TIME

One day at a time – I learned that in recovery and from God. The Lord gives us a daily reprieve. I have learned and am still learning not to listen to the lies of the enemy. Listen to our Father in Heaven. We so blessed today. Just for today. We are forgiven of yesterday, all the blunders and screw-ups. He forgives us. We don't always forgive ourselves. Tomorrow is not here yet. If we have food, shelter, nice clean clothes, the rest is all a blessing from God. Every day I try to write ten things I am grateful for. Plus I love to write, so I have a journal to write in. I write to God sometimes. A lot people who have spouses should be grateful for them. They should tell them every day how much they mean to them. The children should be grateful for their parents or parent. We all can live an attitude of gratitude every day. We live in a world that thinks everyone owes them a living or the government owes them. The only one that owes us a living is ourselves, and we get to ask God for his help. He will be there at the drop of a hat. He promised us He would never leave you or forsake you.

A MIRACLE

I have seen the power of God work in my life and others' lives. I have seen miracles, the things that God has done. It is a beautiful thing when you can be a part of that. One day I went to Java City, a well-known coffee shop in Sacramento, California with my friend. She wanted to go to church with me that day so I drove her to the church in my little truck. When we got to church the Holy Spirit started hitting her hard. She tried to leave a couple of times. Some of the people in the church kept her there. The Holy Spirit hit me, too. I went to the altar to pray and she went to the alter with me. I prayed and the Holy Spirit told me to lay hands on her. Oh my God, I saw and felt a shower of light come down on me. I felt it go into her as I was praying and laying hands on her. She gave her heart to the Lord right there at the altar that day. I did not know that two weeks later she would pass away. The Lord works in mysterious ways. I get to be a part of it.

DIFFERENT PLACES

When I traveled around the country I hitchhiked and rode trains all over the place. I stayed at a lot of free places. They called them union gospel missions. You could stay the night and get a meal. Sometimes I would stay at the Salvation Armies, too. These places were a refuge for street people, winos and crazies. Sometimes we would eat like kings, other times you were lucky to get a bowl of soup and a piece of bread. Sometimes they would give you oatmeal or stale doughnuts. It was horrible sometimes, but it was free. Sometimes on the streets, people would pay for my meal at a restaurant. Most of the time, if I got any money it was to drink and smoke cigarettes. Around the holidays they would feed us so much food. I can remember standing or sitting and waiting for the places to open up. There was a collection of characters in these gypsies, tramps, thieves, hobos and rubber tramps. We did not get to eat right away. We had to listen to a sermon and singing first, then we could eat. We called the sermon an ear banging. Now today I love hearing the sermons. One time at a mission listening to the sermon, I watched a guy in front of me. There were bugs crawling around in his hair. They were big ones and a lot of them. Another time I was at a Salvation Army and this crazy man was steadily eating crackers with weevils in them. There were a lot of them, too. For years I would check all the crackers I ate. There were a few times I stayed at these missions. They fed you three times a day and you could work there. They gave us some nice clothes. I would stop drinking and get my life together and get back with the Lord. Then the road would start calling me and I would have to go. With some money in my pocket, I would hit the road to travel to a new place.

DUMPSTER DIVING

It is a lot of fun to find stuff for free. You would be surprised what you can find in the trash and what people will throw away. When I was only eight or nine years old, we lived in a low-income neighborhood. Down the street on the way to the school there was a rich apartment complex. That is where I found out about dumpster diving. I would find radios that worked, toys and all kinds of neat stuff. I would put the things I found in the fort that I built. Then when I started hoboing around the country, I found out you could eat some of the things you found. McDonald's or KFC would throw out the food they couldn't sell. I never got sick from eating stuff out of the garbage. We also use to find food in the dumpsters behind grocery stores. I found raw vegetables and canned goods, all eatable stuff. Now they lock up the dumpsters or give away the dented cans, old pastries and outdated goods to the free pantries. Sometimes these days they call the police if you are digging in the trash.

I have found a lot of new stuff in the trash over the years. I can remember when I lived in West Sacramento, California I would collect cans. They were $2 a pound and everyone was collecting them. I wasn't working so I collected cans and bottles and sometimes I would borrow my friends' old panel truck. It was like driving a tractor. I made $100 a week salvaging and selling. Plus, I would find stuff to sell at the yard sales. One time I made $20 and another time I made $300. I had money for nothing, turning trash into cash, gotta love it. A lot of stuff was given to me. It would be funny if the same person who threw the stuff away or gave it to me would buy it back. One time I found a bicycle in one of the curbside pickups. I had a van to collect all the salvage and take it to the scrap yard. Sometimes the flea markets threw away junk that I would pick out of the bins and sell.

People at the church saved their cans and bottles for me. I had a route I followed. They also gave me their yard sale stuff. Basically I have made a living off the trash that people throw out. As they say, one man's trash is another man's treasure. When I had my hauling business, I didn't always have time to sell everything. When I went out of business, I had $3000 worth of stuff to sell. I love making money for free. Every vehicle I have had, I used for picking up salvage and trash. God has taken care of me with other peoples' junk.

THE RED LIGHT DISTRICT TIMES

We all went to Mexico when I was traveling around in the carnival. It was a tradition to go to a place called Boys Town. It was a little town right at the Texas border. I was 20 years old at the time, when about four of us went there. This little town had a red light district. Every cab driver, kid and whoever lived in Mexico knew where Boys Town was. They had dancing girls, saloons, bars, places to eat and a lot of places had shows. Women on stage were doing all kinds of things. One smoked a cigar, well, use your imagination. Wow, what a show. I got a beer and picked out a hooker. That was the reason why we went, to get laid. We also took a wild cab ride to get there. It was nighttime. We got into the cab and he drove fast. He took the short cuts through allies, around buses and cars. I think people and kids and even a few chickens were trying to get out of the way. We got out of the cab and gave him a tip for getting us there alive. He asked us if we wanted a ride back later. We said no thanks. That was one wild ride.

WOMEN

I have slept with a lot of women in my time, 22 women to be exact. The sad thing is that I have only had two serious relationships. I have missed opportunities to sleep with 40 different women, so I could have been with more. I have almost been married twice. One lady who wanted to marry me would say, "Are we getting married Sunday?" I would say, "No, someday." Some women gave me money. One gave me her check, watches, rings, clothes. One even bought my car when we broke up. The Lord has forgiven me and I have forgiven myself. God will forgive you of your past just like me. Don't wait to clean up. Let him clean you up. Give him your darkest deepest secret. He will put it in the sea of forgiveness forever.

FAST TRAINS

One time I was on the train in Texas, in between El Paso and San Antonio out in the middle of nowhere. The night before we were in Mexico, so we still had a lot of tequila in us and cheap cigarettes. We were feeling no pain, riding in this boxcar at night. It was going so fast I thought it was going to derail or fly off the track. I bet we were going about 90 or 100 mph. The train company in Texas was Missouri Pacific. We used to ride

with Burlington Northern and Southern Pacific. They did not care if you rode their trains; it was the railroad police that gave us the most trouble. They could put you in jail. Some tramps got their stuff taken and burned, or even beaten up. That's why when we caught a train or got off the train, we all would have to do it as it was leaving the yard. Some tramps would throw their stuff on the train, then they could not catch up with the train so their stuff would take off. Some would get caught under the train or fall on the tracks. It was very dangerous hopping trains. One train we did not catch was Union Pacific. If they caught you on the train, they would take you to jail for 90 days.

So this night in Texas, the train was flying down the tracks when all of a sudden it stopped. Breaks were shrieking and you could hear all the train cars slamming together from the sudden stop. That is why we put railroad spikes in the boxcar door – with a sudden stop the open door of boxcars had been known to slam shut and suffocate people. When the train finally came to a stop, we guessed there were some illegal aliens on the train a few boxcars behind us. We heard the border patrol yelling in Spanish then we heard gunshots. But while we were stopped some other illegal aliens tried to hop in our boxcar. We already had five people in there and did not want them riding with us. They were known to be thieves, robbers, even murderers. So we did the only thing we'd learned how to do. We kicked them off our boxcar. It looked like a riot on the train, swinging and hitting until we knocked them out of the boxcar. It looked like something in a movie. We use to carry flares with us for safety, but never used them

NO GAS

One night when I was driving taxi in Sacramento, I picked up two guys and a woman from a bar about 12:30 am. I could not believe what happened next. I ran out of gas on the way to their house. I found out people get angry when you run out of gas. All of a sudden they started yelling at me and threatened to kick my ass. I used to carry a flashlight for finding addresses. It also made a good protector. I pulled that flashlight out and started hollering at them. They calmed down quick. They also paid the meter and apologized for threatening me. I guess they thought the cab driver was crazy. I have been called that before I finally got some gas. Never did that again. God gives us wisdom and knowledge if I ask Him to.

SUNRISE ON THE TRAIN

Arizona is one of the most beautiful states. I love the desert, the wide-open spaces, the sand, the view. I don't like the desert in the wintertime. I was riding on the back of a grain car. I was in my sleeping bag. Just as I woke up, there was the sunrise. Orange and pink skies, it looked like fire. The mountains looked purple. It was breathtaking. It was one of those moments that make you glad to be alive. I just felt like I wanted to ride the freight trains forever. Those moments of living the dream were why I did so much traveling. I would never have found those moments or great times staying in one place. Every day I can see God's beauty and I can be glad to be alive.

GRAPE PICKING

We found out what hard work grape picking is. Pickers don't make a lot of money, at least at the place we got hired on. By the time we bought food, booze and cigarettes, we were broke. We would have ended up owing them, paying them to work. Like that song goes, I can't go Saint Peter because I owe my soul to the company store. Plus in the grape vineyard, we were the only white people that were crazy enough to work there. My friend and I were bumming around and broke. So we decided to start working at a grape farm in Modesto, California. A big bus picked us up and drove us to the fields. I think we lasted a couple of days, maybe a week. We realized we were getting ripped off and it was too hard of work. So we left on foot, way out in the country, about 10 miles from the freeway. So we walked and walked and walked some more. It was night and we were walking down the country road, no lights. We saw a farmhouse with no fences around it. All of a sudden all hell broke loose. In the darkness a pack of dogs started at us. There were five of them but it seemed like twenty. I don't know what happened, but the hair on my back and neck stood up. Fear gripped me but then my fear turned into anger. I started yelling at the top of my lungs. I cussed at those dogs. Those dogs thought I was crazy and they ran away. Then the farmer came out of his house and he started yelling at the dogs. God was watching out for us again. Those dogs could of torn us up.

PERSONALITIES

Over the course of many years I have not loved myself very much. I tend to harm myself, missed many opportunities to prosper. Sometimes I leave before the miracle. I have left when I should have stayed and stayed when I should have left. I think about all the crazy things I have done to myself and the crazy places I wound up. With the crazy thinking sometimes I feel like I am going to go insane, if it was not for God. If not for a lot of prayer, I would need medication. I have had other people tell me that I am crazy, not right in the head. For years I did not like myself, so I would take on other people's character and personalities – movie stars, business leaders, millionaires and billionaires, my friends, even my family. That

makes for a wacko mind. I wondered why I would get confused and angry, stressed out because I was trying to be someone I was not. Personality disorder. I have only taken medication two times. I am trying to love myself today, and God loves me. My friends and family love me. Wherever I go, there are people who love me, too. With the Lord's help and a lot of prayer and writing, one day at a time, I don't have to suffer from anxiety, depression, anger, hatred, panic attacks and fits of rage. We can pray for healing. These are the fruits of the spirit. Every day is a battle. We get to put on the armor of God.

ROUND TRIP TICKET

On another road trip on the train, I left Sacramento to go to Fallbrook, California. I packed up everything in a huge suitcase. It was more like a rolling trunk. Oh my God, it was heavy. I almost broke my back trying to get on and off the train. I met my brother David at the station about 9:00 pm. I had not seen him in 17 years. I forgot what he looked like. That is a long time not to see your brother. We got some dinner before we drove to the house. I got to meet his wife Nina and their family. Well, I moved in with them. The first few months were great. I rested and felt like I was in paradise under the blue skies. We ate at a lot of casino buffets and my brother is a chef, so I was eating well and getting larger. Then the landlady found out I was living there. She gave me a day to leave. I stayed at the motel a day and in the church's backroom on the couch for a couple of days. Then I moved in with one of my brother's friends.

In the first couple of weeks I moved there, I got a job helping an old lady who had a ranch. She always needed something cleaned or something fixed or something thrown away in the dumpster. I helped the guy

that I had moved in with fix his mobile home up for room and board. I was still working for the other lady once in a while. The mobile home had been lived in by a family for 40 years. They did not throw anything away either. This place was a hauler's dream. He thought a lot of it was treasure but it was junk. I had a little room that they had made out of the back porch. He had two little dogs that peed on that carpet for years and I had to tape up the windows so I could not smell the pee and poop. I helped him for about a month then we had a disagreement and I was out of there. I got a motel for a couple of days. After I checked out of the motel, I realized I was really homeless for the first time in a long time. I have been homeless a lot, I just did not know it. I did not consider living in cars, motels, on floors and couches homeless. I had no work, no car, no wife, no family. The lady at the ranch let me stay there in a storage container but the wood was rotten. It smelled so bad that after two days I was back in the motel. The sad thing was I had $2,000 in savings. I did not want to spend it all on rent. I was homeless with $2,000 in the bank. That is insane or crazy. I have been accused of both. Plus I was riding a bicycle everywhere. The lady with the ranch ran out of work, so I went to parking lots at grocery stores and asked people it they needed their windows washed on their vehicles. I made $55 one day, another I made $35. I did not get rich but I made enough to get a motel. Then I realized things were not working out there, so I stayed outside on the couch at her ranch outside. There were coyotes roaming around sometimes.

God was watching over me. My brother David took me to the train station, where some lady and I almost had a confrontation over the bathrooms. Cops showed up. I almost did not leave on the train. I went back to Sacramento, California on another adventure. I won't know why I took that trip until years later. God works in mysterious ways.

FRUGAL LIVING

When you look in the dictionary you see my picture in there under frugal. I hate to say it but I hate spending money. I have had a lot of vehicles and they all made me money. I have even lived in a lot of them. I had a van one time, oh my God it ate so much gas. It was a four-barrel carburetor, 460 engine, one-ton Ford E-450 Econoline. I bought it for $800 and made $2000 with it, hauling and doing flea market and yard sales. I have always bought stuff for cheap, turned around and sold them later. Now in my Christian walk I like to give things away. I am frugal but I am a giver. He put that in my heart. I don't always make money off vehicles. Some I had to junk. I sold the van for $350. I have had lots of stuff I needed to throw away or give away. Sometimes I give it to the trashcan. I have learned how to wear one pair of pants or one shirt. Then they get too bad to wear. You learn to wear them and throw them away. I have been a survivor my whole life. The Lord Jesus was a survivor, too. He was born in an animal stable. He was homeless more than people think. He said that the Son of Man has nowhere to lay his head. He was a hobo, too.

CARNIVAL DAYS

When I first joined the carnival I thought I found Heaven. I could travel and make tons of money. We made some really good money and spent it like rock stars. There were a lot of women and we all had a lot of fun. We traveled all over the US and I loved it. In some places we would stay at a nice hotel and the next place we would live in the cars, under the trucks, in tents and sleeping bags. We played in little towns, big cities and state fairs. It was a lot of work though. We would set up the tents tear them down, then drive to the next spot. We worked 12 to 14 hours a day. The problem was, we did a lot of drugs and alcohol, all the time. That is why I left. There were too many drugs and you burned out quick. I bet you didn't know that carnies have their own language. People that work the booth are called jointies and people working the rides are called ride jocks.

HOMELESSNESS

I was staying in Kalispell, Montana when my brother's wife and I got in an argument. They kicked me out of the house and once more I was back on the streets with no home. I found out where the free places to eat were. Kalispell has a lot of good places to eat for free. There is a certain freedom in being homeless, just like on the road or traveling. There is a loneliness, an emptiness, sometimes fear. There is the uncertainty of someone stealing your stuff or beating you up in your sleeping bag. There's weather, animals, spiders, bugs banging into your head – even the sprinklers coming on or someone pissing on you or crazy people. One time, I hit my head on the side of a building and gave myself a concussion. You can't think about all the things that might happen or you will never sleep. Plus there is an evil spirit out there on the streets.

I have met a lot of neat people in Montana. It is one of my favorite places to stay. One of my best friends in Montana was Jack. What a character. He used to be a Mercedes Benz car salesman. He loved women and gambling. Some other people I have in known in Montana were these ladies who did a blog on me that is worth the read. After the blog I left Montana for five months. I always miss Montana when I am gone and can't wait to get back there. You will only understand if you live there or visit. You will never be the same. The people are friendly and my family lives in Montana, too. I love my mom Carlyne no matter how many places I have been. I still like to travel. Like I said in a few chapters, the Lord made me a hobo. I love it.

BUGS AND ANIMALS

I have been bitten twice by black widows. They make you very sick and you can hallucinate from the poison. I was either bitten by a family of spiders or one big spider. I did not go to the doctor, just used antibiotic ointment. The spider bites were gone in a couple of weeks. I have been bitten by chiggers and ticks. You are exposed to a lot of critters when you are sleeping outside. I was living under the bridge next to the train tracks.

It was October, just starting to get cool at night. About 3:00 in the morning I heard a bunch of coyotes off in the distant. The sound started getting louder. I got nervous. All I had to fight off the coyotes with was a hickory cane and a small knife. If I took a few out, the rest would be having me for dinner. So I decided to get out of there quick. As I rolled up my sleeping bag, I looked behind me to make sure they were not biting me. I believe that was the Holy Spirit telling me to get out of there. Sometimes I listen and sometimes I don't. I am better off when I do.

THE SANDWICH MINISTRY

It all started with a hamburger and a cup of coffee and prayer. Then I bought 25 hamburgers and gave them away. It was the best feeling, helping and feeding the street people. I was on the streets too at the time. Then I got a loaf of bread and some mayonnaise and bologna. I made the sandwiches and I rode my bicycle to give the sandwiches out to street people. I have seen miracles and healing. I prayed for a man one day. His legs and feet were so swollen up that he could not walk. I laid hands on him and prayed. The next day he was walking around and his legs were skinny. I got to go right into the homeless camps. I went up and down the streets every day and to the bus stops, bringing some people to Christ. Others poured out their hearts to me and told their stories. One lady was even crying. Sometimes I prayed for them. Sometimes I just listened. What a blessing that I had that ministry. God is great.

KEEPING IT SIMPLE

I love the idea of keeping it simple, and that's what I have done while living on the streets. Even before that, life was pretty simple except when I was in business for myself. Then things can get complicated with deadlines, appointments, bids, employees, finishing the job on time and doing the job right. These days I really don't want much – maybe a bicycle, a dog and a wife. Maybe a motel or a place that is safe. I can live off of $3500 a year. It gives me such peace that I don't need to have all these toys like houses or cars. I don't even want a car right now. I am enjoying my time on the streets. I like that I get to pray for others and lead them to Christ. I like not being tied down to one place, unlike people who are settling down and growing roots. We used to hear that in recovery, KISS: Keep it simple, stupid. I don't like anyone calling me stupid. I used to say to people, "Keep it stupid, simple."

I get to see the beautiful sunrises and sunsets, God's artwork. We are God's artwork, too. I enjoy green grass, blooming trees in the spring and a good thunderstorm, as long as I am under cover. Last night I slept on a picnic table under a big tent while a thunderstorm raged all around me. The trees are blooming, there's no more snow, the nights are warmer and the days are hotter. The mountains up here are beautiful. It's tourist season in Montana and the motor homes are starting to show up. The prices of motels will skyrocket. I am a snowbird. I hate the cold, so come winter and hell or high water, I am leaving for Las Vegas, California or Arizona. I'll come back in the summer. Next year I might visit the East Coast, then go to Alaska or Hawaii. Then I will have seen all of the United States. That's why I am the rich hobo – I get to see all these places. It is a miracle of God. He takes care of me so well.

LEARNING TO LIVE INSIDE

I've been homeless since 2008. I think I've been homeless off and on since I was 18 years old and now I have a place at the age of 55. Over the years, I've stayed in all kinds of different places, even a meat locker. It had a heater and a bed. It was paradise. I was inside for the winter. I have just

found a place to live. It takes a while to adjust from living on the streets, on the ground, out in the elements and with the spiders. It was getting so cold at night waiting for 9:00 so I could bed down and get warm. I have an Army mummy bag good for -20 below. I realized the other night that they make up two sheets into the bed, a top sheet and a bottom. I haven't slept in sheets for years, except in motels. I stayed at a lady's house from church and she had a bed with two sheets. I told that story to my friends and they had a good laugh. People don't understand how hard it is to transition into inside living. Inside is so much better than outside. Maybe it's like a disease or sickness that haunts us. You get used to that way of living outside on the streets and pretty soon you start liking it. You can come and go as you please. There's a lot of mental illness on the streets, crazies, people always ready to fight. There are some nice people on the streets, too.

I have a feeling deep down that God does not want us to live like that, almost like animals. We are champions in His eyes. We are winners. He wants us to enjoy our lives, enjoy others and have others enjoy us, breaking bread together. I am still learning how to adjust to this new way of living. I enjoy a shower every night, a warm bed and a roof over my head. God is so good all the time.

FLAGS

A funny thing is that as I am writing this book, I am still selling my wares. I sell books to a book dealer. I sell hats and jackets, whatever I can find. Most of the time I sell little 4 x 6 inch flags for a dollar each that I buy wholesale. The newspaper in Kalispell wrote an article about me and my small business. They left out some of the things I told them and didn't write my whole story, but it is worth a read. At the time of the article, I complained about how people treat the homeless. Instead, I should have been thanking those who have blessed me in the last year. We have to trust God in all things.

Some days selling flags I have only made $4 and some days zero. Between the bad days and the good, I make about $10 an hour after taxes. Yes, I pay taxes and have a vending license. I sell for a living, but I think I love writing more. Selling is a rough way to make a living and I wish people were nicer to me. I am trying to do the best I can. I work 24 to 26 hours a week, and it feels more like 40 or 50 hours. My body is messed up, so is my mind sometimes. People act like I am doing something wrong. I wish they would treat me like a human being. I feel so bad out there selling my wares sometimes. It is sad when people act like that. I still like selling a good product for a good price. I am not lazy; I am a flag salesman. This country was built by entrepreneurs, salespeople and street vendors. God bless all of us.

KINDNESS

It is very hard sometimes to show kindness in this world. It is not a kind and gentle world we live in. There is a lot of noise, computers, TV's and crazy people. There are some mean people out there that just don't care about anything but themselves. I know from experience and have been on both sides of it. I am not perfect by far. The only one who is perfect is Jesus Christ.

As I sell my flags on corners where the traffic is, people stop for the light, and I have 30 seconds, sometimes more, sometimes less to get their attention. I put little stickers on the flags, like God Loves U, Smile U Are Blessed, You Are a Champion, You Are Special, God Bless You, King of Kings, Smile Jesus Loves U, Soar with the Eagles and Jesus is Lord. I ask a dollar for a flag and sometimes people give me more. The people who buy the flags are very nice. They are happy to buy a flag or just to give. Sometimes they wave their flag. I've found out that those who buy the flags are happier than those who don't. There are mad and rude people out there. I see them every day except Sunday.

Kindness goes a long way in the world of anger, noise and stress. I am learning how to be kind to others and to myself. It is not easy to be kind to people that are treating you like dirt. I want to yell and curse at them, and I have. I ask for God's forgiveness and repent daily. I try to remember this scripture from Matthew 22:37, "Love the Lord your God with all your heart and with all your soul and with all your mind. This is the first and greatest commandment. And the second is like it: Love your neighbor as yourself. All the law and prophets hang on these two commandments."

SADNESS IN THE USA

It has been about eight months since I have written anything. I am still selling flags. I have a new line of products – big American flags, Montana State flags, P.O.W.'s, Marine and Christian flags, flag pins and walking sticks in the summer. I sell business to business, too. For the most part, businesses are nice to me. They buy my flags. They trust me, and like me and my product. The sadness in the USA is that it's the only place where people get mad at a person for selling flags. That is how I make my living. I don't get a disability check, no food stamps and don't eat at free food places. I make my living from selling my wares on the street corners and make sales to people in the parking lots. People can get so angry at others who sell things, especially if you are vending on the corner. Then I get angry back at them. I shouldn't be angry, I should be praying for them and I do.

There are some days I can sell flags for five hours; other days I can only sell for two. I do what I can. I am proud of my little business that has been growing. I started when I was on the streets, in August of 2015.

The Life & Times of the Rich Hobo

I was homeless and selling pens and pencils, two for a dollar. I did little yard sales and sold books until I made enough to buy some flags. I pan-handled for a month until the Lord told me I should sell my flags only and not panhandle any more. He promised to take care of me and he has. One day I was selling flags in a blizzard and I made $158 in a half hour. Another time in was only 10 degrees and a lady gave me $120. There are nice people out there, and the ones who buy my flags make up for those who don't. I sell at all the parades, too. I love parades – a lot of people to sell to all in one place. I made $1000 one day at two parades. I even hired a security person and a sales person. The Lord will feed the little birds in the air. How much more will he take care of you.

I like not having a job, no boss to tell me when to come in, when to leave or when to wake up. It is a working prison unless you love what you are doing. Most jobs I had I hated, or loved them at first and then I grew to hate them. I burned out on jobs. Now I can't work much, I am a wreck physically. Work has to be something I love. You are living the dream when you are doing things you love to do. God is love.

FAMILY

Well, you can imagine how family can be after years of hoboing all over the country. Some of my family disapproves of my life style. To this day I am sad because most of my family does not want me to visit or stay around. Some of them did not invite me to their family reunion. I was on the train for four days and got in at 9:00 pm. That is a tough time to get a motel. That is why this country is in trouble – there is no more family. I forgive them the best I can, in Jesus' name. God bless them. If you have a family member like me, treat them like you love them, just like Jesus would. Jesus said, for the least of these that you have given water, food, clothing, housing, visited them in the hospitals or jails, you have done it unto Me. When you give to the poor, you give unto the Lord.

TO FLORIDA AND BACK

I started out in Montana and caught the bus in Kalispell in late Sept. 2014. The first part of the bus ride was not bad, three days and two nights. My legs and feet swelled up three times their normal size and it took a couple of days for the swelling to go down. I stayed in for five months. I went through the worst weather a homeless person can endure – thunderstorms, hail, snow, ice, wind and rain. Fifteen below zero on a bicycle is pretty cold. With the wind, it might have been 25 below. I was bit by spiders one night eleven times. A nice lady let me stay out of the freezing cold behind her antique shop in a storage building. The Lord blesses me with people like that all the time. Plus she used to give me money. I think she adopted me as her son who had been on the streets, too. He committed suicide. So sad, but the streets will do that to you. A lot of evil spirits and demonic forces are out there on the streets. That life steals, robs, destroys, kills, just like the enemy who is a liar, cheat and thief.

So I had enough of the cold weather and rude people, including myself. I got a train ticket to Florida from Topeka, Kansas to Chicago to Washington DC then Jacksonville, Florida. I stayed in Saint Augustine, Florida for a month. It was nice weather, I had some fun and met some nice people. I also met a lot of rude people, rude drivers. People were not happy. So there I was again, riding the train for four days and burnt out. I was heading back to Montana to try starting over again. Life is a lot of start overs. I might leave Montana and start over again, or I might just keep traveling. It makes it hard to go back to a place where you are not welcomed by your family. We all have such a short time here. You would think we would all get along better. Be more loving, kind and patient – all the things I am working on, too, every day. Living from day to day, you are looked upon like scum, a bum, a leper, a person with a disease. If it was not for God in my life, I would have committed suicide a few times. Just a couple of months ago I was so mad that I was ready to throw my bike over the bridge and was going on over, too. That is what I call a meltdown. I am going to see some old friends. I am glad that I still have some old hobo friends and church family. I saw my friends Larry and Darcy. They are mighty prayer warriors. It was good to see them again.

THE LORD'S BLESSING IN YOUR LIFE

Memorize the scriptures in the Bible, etch them in your mind and accept a blessing each day. One day at a time. Deuteronomy 28:3 – You will be blessed in the city and in the country. Deuteronomy 28:6 – You will be blessed when you come in and in your going out. Deuteronomy 28:8 – The Lord will send you a blessing on your barns and everything you put your hands to. Deuteronomy 28:11 – The Lord will grant you abundant prosperity. Deuteronomy 28:12 – The Lord will open the heavens, the storehouse of his bounty, to send rain in season and to bless all the work of your hands. You will lend to many nations but borrow from none. Deuteronomy 28:13 – The Lord will make you the head, not the tail. Joshua 1:6 – Be strong and courageous. Joshua 1:7 – Be strong and very courageous, that you may be successful wherever you may go. Job 36:11 – If they obey and serve him they will spend the rest of their days in prosperity and their years in contentment.

Isaiah 43:18 – Forget the former things, do not dwell on the past. See that I am doing a new thing. Matthew 25:15 – The man who had received the five talents went at once and put his money to work and gained five more. Psalms 30:2 – O Lord my God, I called to you for help and you healed me. Psalms 46:1 – God is our strength to the weary and the power of the weak. Even the youths grow tired and weary and young men stumble and fall but those who hope in the Lord will renew their strength. They will soar on wings like eagles, they will run and not be weary, they will walk and not be faint. Matthew 8:20 – Foxes have holes and the birds of the air nests, but the Son of Man has nowhere to lay his head. Psalms 1:3 – Whatever he does prospers. Psalms 34:4 – I sought the Lord and he answered me. He delivered me from all my fears. Psalms 34:6 – This poor man called and the Lord heard him, he saved him out of all his troubles. Psalms 34:7 – The angel of the Lord triumphs around those who fear him and delivers them. Psalm 37:3 – Trust in the Lord and do good, dwell in the land and enjoy safe pasture. Delight yourself in the Lord and He will give you the desires of your heart. Proverbs 10:22 – The blessings of the Lord bring wealth and add no trouble to it. Proverbs 11:2 – A generous man will prosper, he who refreshes others will himself be refreshed. Proverbs 13:22 A good man leaves an inheritance for his children's children. Luke 6:38 – Give and it will be given to you. A good measure, pressed down, shaken together and running over will be poured into your lap. For with the measure you use, it will be measured to you. Luke 17:19 – Then He said to him, rise and go. Your faith has made you well. Acts 20:35 – It is more blessed to give than to receive. Romans 8:31 – If God is for us, who can be against us? Romans 8:37 – In all these things we are more than conquerors through Him who loved us.

I know these scriptures will bless you. I know they have blessed me.

by Allen L. Wellenstein

God willing, I hope my stories have touched your life. The main thing I hope is that God and the Lord Jesus Christ have touched your life. I hope the stories have been an adventure to read. What a journey and there is more to come; it will be in other books. I had fun writing this book. It brought a lot of memories and thought reflections. I feel no regret, guilt or anger about things of the past. All we have is today. Through ups and downs always remember that God loves you. There are so many good things in life if we look for them. We always find what we are looking for. God bless you.

I will see you down the road.
Al Wellenstein, The Rich Hobo

17146203R00052

Made in the USA
Lexington, KY
17 November 2018